LIVING
OFF THE GRID

The Essential Guide to Embracing
Minimalism and Self Reliance with Your
Own Sustainable Homestead

CHASE BOURN

Contents

Introduction

THERE IS A huge problem staring you in the face every day. You wake up to your blaring alarm clock, commute to a job that you hate in a fancy car that you detest paying for, just to make money for someone else.

You're tired of our modern, complicated society, piles of bills, and the lack of freedom your current situation is bringing you. You dream of that cute little hobby farm or that minimalist homestead where you are actually contributing to the Earth rather than taking away from it. There is an Eco-warrior inside you just begging to get out and live a pollution-free and sustainable life that is full of choices and the freedom to do what you want.

Wouldn't it be great if you just had a guide to show you exactly how to transition into living off-grid and being self-reliant?

That is exactly what this book is all about!

This book will be your complete guide to everything you need to know to transition to living off-grid and establishing a self-reliant, sustainable, and eco-friendly life. I am going to outline everything you need to know from obtaining the right job to how to set up your off-grid electrical system and so much more!

But before we jump into that, I want to introduce myself.

My name is Chase Bourn, and I have been living off-grid for over seven years now on over 10 acres of land that I own. For the past seven years, I have been living my dream of self-reliance through a very minimalistic and eco-friendly lifestyle. Although in the grand scheme of things, seven years doesn't seem like a very long time, in that time I have gained a lifetime of knowledge and experience that I want to pass on to you. There is a lot to learn when going off-grid and I want to share the things that I have learned with you to make your transition easier and more successful.

You see, I can't even begin to explain how happy I am with my lifestyle choice. Every day I wake up (without an alarm clock) and am able to take in the beauty of my off-grid homestead that I have personally created. Heck, my closest neighbor is several miles away.

I am literally living out a dream that I had several years ago that I originally never thought was possible to achieve. Now, I couldn't be happier.

Over the last couple of years, I have personally helped hundreds of people successfully make the transition to the off-grid lifestyle. It is my hope that I am able to help thousands of more people through this book. Even now, I receive weekly messages, emails, and even some snail mail to my PO Box from people thanking me for helping them with their transition, which makes me feel great!

I'm going to make you a promise with this book... If you take this book and fully digest every chapter, you are going to be fully equipped and empowered to change your life from the 9-5 grind to living in your own serene paradise. Even if you don't have any experience in off-grid living, all you need is the desire to do so and the knowledge of everything there is to learn from this book. Think of this book as the first tool in your toolbox.

Stop putting it off!

If you truly want to live this life then stop putting it off, stop saying *"Someday I'll do it..."* and start putting that "someday" plan into action now. I'm sure you know all too well what happens to people who keep saying "someday," that day never comes and they live their lives in regret. They regret that they were never brave enough to go after their dreams and then end up saying *"I wish I would have..."*. So take that leap of faith and use this manual as your road map to achieve your off-grid living goals.

This Off-Grid Living Manual will take you by the hand and show you step-by-step everything that you need to start living a life of freedom off-grid. I can't emphasize enough the joy and satisfaction I experience living my sustainable and off-grid lifestyle. It is truly a free way to live and it's all outlined for you here in this book.

You might already be asking these questions:

- *How will I make money?*
- *Where will I live?*
- *What about water and electricity?*

No worries, I cover all of that and more in great depth for you in this book.

Here is just a small sample of the topics I will cover in this book:

- The different types of off-grid living
- Is off-grid living really for you?
- How to embrace minimalism
- Getting your finances in order
- Where to buy property
- Formulating your plan
- Everything you need to know about water - from storage to sewage
- Multiple types of alternative power sources
- How to reduce your energy consumption
- How to communicate with the outside world (living off-grid doesn't mean you need to be a hermit, unless you want to)

- ☒ Self-sustaining food systems
- ☒ Keeping your homestead safe
- ☒ And how to make money living off-grid

Keep reading and you will be a master at off-grid, sustainable living in no time!

CHAPTER ONE:
What Is Off-Grid Living All About?

WHILE MANY PEOPLE dream of living off-grid, it is certainly not a lifestyle that everyone can acclimate to. It takes a lot of knowledge, determination, and planning to be able to live off the grid successfully.

In this chapter, I am going to share with you a bit of my story and how I came to be the expert homesteader I am today and the different types of off-grid or homesteading situations. Plus, I'll give you a little peek into the reality of the off-grid lifestyle so that you can determine if you are going to be cut out for an off-grid lifestyle and if the off-grid lifestyle is right for you.

The Story Of Chase Bourn

It was about eight years ago. I was working a corporate job that I dreaded going to every day. I quickly began to realize that what I thought I wanted - the big fancy job, the expensive car, and the downtown apartment - was exactly what I had become. I felt like I was living in the movie *Groundhog Day*, where it is the same day over and over again. I was just going through the motions.

My health was declining from eating out all the time and being too busy to cook a decent meal. I felt like the pollution in the city was suffocating me more and more every day. While I was good at my job and was paid pretty well, I just felt unfulfilled and empty. I wasn't really making a difference. I was a number cruncher, a thousand other people in the city could have probably done my job.

I started reading self-improvement books in an effort to try and "find" myself, but nothing seemed to speak to me. Then one day I was trying this new mindset meditation and realized something profound. It was a guided meditation and the soft, serene voice told me to visualize what my ideal day looked like and how I would feel experiencing such an ideal day. Then the soothing voice guided me into meditating on how this ideal day fit into my overall ideally imagined life.

I realized at that moment that I was not living my ideal day or my ideal life. My ideal life was one where I was unplugged, living off of the land, and being the eco-warrior I always knew I was in my heart. Some call it being a hippie, I call it being conscious.

In my ideal life, I would be able to wake up every day feeling complete and satisfied with the life I had built for myself. I would not ever have to worry about waking up to that annoying alarm clock. Instead, I would be able to pour my cup of freshly brewed coffee, sit on my back porch and be able to take in all that nature has to offer without having to worry about rushing off to work and sitting in traffic. I would be able to live and work on my own terms without having to rely on society to fulfill my needs.

From that day on I made a mindset shift.

I wasn't going to be trapped in the 9-5 job that I hated any longer. I was going to do everything in my power to make that perfect day that I saw in my mind a reality. I scoured every corner of the internet, book stores, and libraries. I went to meetups and seminars. I did anything and everything possible to get more information on how to successfully live off-grid.

It wasn't easy. It took a lot of trial and error, but I finally did it. I was able to transition out of my toxic city life and into my ideal life. I now wake up every morning feeling fulfilled and happy to be alive. And I want to share my passion with you in hopes that you will realize your dream and cut your binding ties to the all too busy world and begin to live life on your own terms.

The Different Types Of Off-Grid Living

I'm sure you already know by now what off-grid living is or, at least, have an idea about what it is. The goal of being off-grid is to have autonomy; you provide your own water, sewer, gas, electric, and any other utilities without the help of outside companies. While many people view off-grid living as breaking from the dependence of all utilities, traditionally it refers to living off of the electrical grid. Generally speaking, there are three different kinds of off-grid living: truly roughing it (you might as well just be camping), the half-on/half-off lifestyle, and the modern off-grid lifestyle.

Roughing it

This type of off-grid living is not for the faint of heart. While it certainly is the cheapest form of off-grid living, they don't call it roughing it for nothing! Those that rough it often don't have access to running water in their dwelling, which is called a "dry cabin."

Think pioneer days here!

The roughing it type of off-grid living does not hook up to any kind of electrical grid either, and generally includes an outhouse and probably a small garden or homestead. Any power obtained would be from a generator, nights would be lit by candlelight, and you would get plenty of exercise having to haul your water from the nearest stream or lake. While you could certainly collect rainwater, there comes a cost with that as well. Generally, individuals that seek the roughing-it lifestyle are looking to spend as little as possible.

Without access to running water, you would have to wash your clothes by hand (or stash a lot of coins for a laundry mat) and rig up an outdoor shower. Although this doesn't guarantee hot water either, so you should get used to taking cold showers. You must also find alternative methods for cooking, like over an open fire, and ways to refrigerate food as well that don't require electricity. If this is the kind of lifestyle you are serious about, try camping for an extended period of time first to see if it is right for you.

Half on / half off

This is one of the most popular methods of off-grid living that many people have chosen to adopt. This is also a great way for people to start if they are wanting to homestead and become self-sufficient. You can live the off-grid lifestyle while still enjoying some of the modern amenities like hot running water.

Many individuals that do half on/half off rely on their nearby city for some of their utilities, most commonly electrical. Many homes in the country, such as farms and homesteads, already have wells and septic tanks so they are considered off-grid for those utilities. If you are building a home, you can get a well and a septic tank for a fairly affordable price.

Other than how you get your utilities, most other daily living activities are the same. You can still cook a meal on a gas stove or plug in your computer to work from home (more on that in Chapter 10). While there are many people who might not consider this type of lifestyle off-grid, it is a great way to transition into a more off-grid lifestyle and get started. Plus, it beats living in the city!

Modern off-grid lifestyle

Many people are opting for the modern off-grid lifestyle in which they are able to have all of their modern amenities but do not rely on utility companies for anything. Being totally off-grid by no means translates into "roughing it" in this case. Simply put, you are your own power supply. With modern off-grid living you can still retain all of the luxuries that life in the city holds, but on your own terms. Modern off-grid living allows you to be in the middle of nowhere - or even in the middle of everything - while only having to rely on yourself.

A modern off-grid home would include an electric-powered well, a septic tank, and either solar panels, wind power, or a hydropower system. Solar energy is becoming increasingly affordable to many people. A company is even working on creating a solar roof that looks just like regular roofing shingles that will help to power your home and your electric car. Due to the way financing solar panels works, it is generally advised that you purchase them without financing or use a home equity line of credit, otherwise you can lose out on a big solar tax credit.

Are You Cut Out For Off-Grid Living?

There are many reasons that people choose to go off-grid, but generally, people choose to go off-grid for the independence that it offers as well as the appeal of not having to pay for utilities for the rest of their lives.

Before you make the jump to off-grid living, you should connect with others that are living off-grid and see how they are doing things. Transitioning to living off-grid is easier for some than others. If you are not looking to sell off all of your belongings and start roughing it, then going off-grid is going to require some initial investment and a lot of planning.

When going off-grid the physical location has a lot to do with your success. Some areas simply do not allow you to go off-grid until you are going solar and installing a well. Another large factor to consider is the initial financial aspect. While roughing it is certainly the cheapest option, many people still prefer modern amenities, like electric lights, running water, and flushing toilets. All of these modern amenities require building a reliable, self-sustaining system, which can be expensive to get started with.

Going off-grid is a big decision. It isn't some fun little hobby that you can try one day and change your mind the next. It is a lifestyle, thus you should make sure that you can commit to it for the long haul. Depending on the level of off-grid you do, you have to consider how your life will change in other aspects. Do you get your groceries delivered to your house now? That's not a likely scenario when you are off-grid. Do you seem to have all of your electrical appliances running at once, all the time? Such as your TV, computer, phone, tablet, etc all plugged in at the same time? This really isn't possible with going off-grid either. You have to be conscious of the energy that you are using and how to save it for when you really need it.

So before you dive headfirst into the whole off-grid lifestyle, take some time to really think about how you are currently living your life and how you actually want to live your life. Make a list of your personal pros and cons and see if the pros outweigh the cons. While I think more people should go off-grid and be self-sufficient on their own homestead, I know that many people are not cut out for this lifestyle, and that's ok. My hope is if you're reading this book that you are saying *"YES!"* to going off-grid and feel as if this is the life you are meant to live!

If so...

Then keep reading! I have so much more in store for you!

Chapter Summary

About eight years ago, while working a corporate job that I hated, I had a mindset shift that changed the course of my life. I decided that I was going to leave my city job and life and live off-grid. With a lot of trial and error, I was able to transition out of my toxic city life into living off-grid on my own terms.

There are several types of off-grid living: roughing it, half-on/half-off, and the modern off-grid lifestyle. Roughing it is the most extreme but frugal option - think of a tent and using leaves for toilet paper.

While the half-on/half-off form of off-grid living is one of the most popular methods of off-grid living. It promotes living off the electrical grid but also maintaining access to some modern amenities such as running water and indoor plumbing.

Modern off-grid living is just like living in a normal house in any city or country. They have access to all of the modern amenities that any on-grid household would have but are disconnected from the electrical grid.

There are many reasons that people choose off-grid living, most commonly for the independence that it offers as well as the appeal of saving a lot of money. Don't be shy about connecting with others that are living off-grid to see how they are doing certain things. Initially, going off-grid does require a lot of planning, investment, and commitment. You want to be sure that you are all in before you make the jump.

In the next chapter, we are going to cover how to actually get started with your transition into off-grid living. It starts with how and what to downsize from your current living situation, how you can embrace the minimalist lifestyle and mentality, and how you can save more money for your off-grid lifestyle.

CHAPTER TWO:
Where And How To Get Started

Great!

Now THAT you have decided that living off-grid is for you, let's dive into all the nuts and bolts about how and where to get started.

Going off-grid is not a decision that should be taken lightly. There is a lot that goes into the decision and a lot that goes into the transition. In this chapter, we are going to go over how to downsize, what you should and should not be getting rid of, how to embrace minimalism, and how to get your finances in order so that you have success from the start.

How And What To Downsize And Get Rid Of All Of Your Junk

The longer you live in a place, the more stuff you tend to collect. Just look at any elderly person that has lived in the same house for 20 to 50 years. They have so much stuff! Stuff they never use. Stuff they forgot they had. Stuff that serves no purpose or no longer brings them joy.

When you go off-grid it is more about the essentials that you need to live and less about trying to keep up with the Joneses and owning the latest new thing. It can be pretty overwhelming trying to get rid of things that you have held onto for years. But trust me, once you take the leap, you will not regret it! It is such a freeing feeling to be able to walk through your home knowing that everything is there for a purpose rather than just because you wanted it. Being able to downsize will make your transition into off-grid living much easier.

It is likely that you have way more things than you actually need - clothes, dishes, trinkets, TVs, shoes, tech gadgets, so on and so on.

I think you get the hint.

While not all off-grid living requires living in a tiny home, you should take that approach when downsizing. The fewer material possessions you have, the less you have to get distracted by, the less stressed out you will be.

Clothing

Take clothing, for example. Look at some of the most well known and successful men in the world - Steve Jobs, Mark Zuckerberg, and Elon Musk. They are not wearing loads of name brand clothing wherever they go. They are wearing basic jeans and t-shirts. Realistically, if you are doing laundry once per week, you only need enough clothes to last you that week, some pajamas, and maybe a few special occasion items.

I'm not saying this just to the men either. It is entirely possible for women to drastically cut down on their wardrobes as well and create what is called a capsule wardrobe. This is where they have a handful of key pieces that they can mix and match into many different outfits. Cutting down on your clothes not only cuts down on the space you need for clothing, but also cuts down on water and electricity to wash everything.

When you are going through all of your clothing, figure out what you want to keep, donate, and toss. For every item that you are keeping, try to get rid of one to three items, this will ensure that you are only keeping what you actually need and aren't bringing clutter into your new off-grid lifestyle. You can certainly try and make some extra cash by selling your gently used clothes online or at a rummage sale. Just make sure to put that extra money you make into your savings!

Tech items & appliances

If you are anything like I was, I always felt that I had to have the latest tech gadgets - smartphones, Bluetooth headphones, tablets, TVs, smartwatches, etc. While this is fine and I totally get that people love the newest tech items, are these really necessary for your new off-grid lifestyle? Not to mention it takes a lot of energy to charge such items.

What about all the appliances that you have?

Kitchen appliances can be a big category. If you haven't already, try and downsize your kitchen appliances and gadgets to the bare essentials. For example, do you really need a special avocado slicer? Probably not, a sharp knife and spoon serve the same purpose and can be used for many other tasks. Keep the kitchen appliances and gadgets that allow you to do multiple things. For example, instead of having a slow cooker and a yogurt maker, get a pressure cooker/multi-pot that allows you to do several cooking functions with only one appliance. There are even combination washer and dryer units that help to save on space and energy as well!

Take a good look at all the tech items and appliances that you own and determine which ones you really need. Having lots of tech items and kitchen appliances eats up a lot of energy and can take time away from personal development activities. Also, opt for energy-efficient appliances whenever possible. Selling the items you no longer want or need can also be a great way to earn some extra money to get your off-grid lifestyle started.

Trinkets/family heirlooms

Parting with family heirlooms can be difficult for many people. If you have a lot of items that were handed down to you it might be time to part with them or pass them on. One option is to hand them down to other family members that might treasure the items. Otherwise, you can take a picture of the item and create a scrapbook that helps to preserve the memories of your special items.

How To Embrace Minimalism

Minimalism has so many benefits other than just having less stuff to trip over in your house. Decluttering your living space can benefit both your physical and mental health. Not only that, decluttering has extended benefits into your interpersonal relationships, finances, health, and general wellbeing.

Minimalism isn't about giving up all of your worldly possessions to live in a tiny house with one pair of socks. Minimalism is all about being able to live a more meaningful life with less stuff in order to focus on health, relationships, passions, growth, and contributing to the larger good. Knowing exactly where to start with the minimalist lifestyle can be rather daunting. Everyone's vision for their minimalist lifestyle looks a little different. You must first be able to determine what your vision looks like.

This is where doing some visioning exercises and meditation can work really well. Think about your *why* for a minute. Why do you want to embrace the minimalist lifestyle? What are your hoping to achieve by doing so?

Are you wanting to get rid of your stuff to free yourself from the clutches of consumerism? Embracing the minimalist lifestyle is as much about your mindset than it is about anything else. It's a shift in your lifestyle and change in habits that run deep within every aspect of your life.

In order to really get started with your minimalist lifestyle, do a lifestyle audit. This is where you start to connect your vision to reality. Take some time to seriously consider every aspect of your life. This includes everything from your life to your daily activities and habits. If possible, do some time tracking of your daily life. What are you actually spending your time on? What do you want to be spending your time on?

It's time, to be honest with yourself. Quit living in denial. Do you really need those movie tickets from your high school sweetheart? Either scrapbook them or get rid of them! It is really an amazing and freeing feeling when you get rid of all the clutter in your home. Draw inspiration from reading books, blogs, and listening to podcasts about minimalism and try and connect with other people that are practicing this lifestyle.

I would not, however, suggest to go through your entire house in a weekend and declutter everything. Start small, with one room or with one group of items. You don't want to be thrown in a tizzy of decluttering and getting rid of something you should have kept or get burnt out and give up on the idea completely.

I've mentioned this a few times, whatever you decide that you want to get rid of, try and sell it for some extra cash to put towards your off-grid lifestyle. It's pretty simple. Once you have a couple of piles of stuff that you want to get rid of, have a yard sale and make a couple extra hundred to a thousand dollars or more.

While you are going through all of your physical items, don't forget about your online digital life as well. Cut back on the five million emails that you get every day. Make a conscious effort to only have the tabs open on your computer that you are actively using. Organize all of your bookmarks and your digital files. Also, don't forget about making an effort to unplug. When you are able to step away from the smartphone or the computer, you give yourself more time to enjoy the things you really want to work on, such as personal development.

Much the same as with a digital decluttering, take a look at all the paper that you accumulate. Magazine subscriptions that you never read, bills that you just throw away because you pay them online, and even paper products that you use in your home like napkins and paper towels. There are literally tons of different ways to switch out everyday paper products for sustainable and reusable options that are not only better for the environment but better for your health as well.

Lastly, one thing to really take into consideration in a truly minimalist lifestyle is to value experiences over material possessions. When you are old and sick your material possessions won't really matter, what will matter are your memories. This is where some meditation and reflection will do you a lot of good in determining what you value the most.

Building Success From The Start: Getting Your Finances In Order

While it's all good and well to declutter your physical and digital space, going off-grid isn't going to happen if you don't have your finances in order. If you have poor money habits, that is not going to change just because you got rid of a bunch of your stuff and are moving off-grid. As with making any big change in your life, your finances should play a role in your mindset shift as well.

One of the things that you do not want to do in going off-grid is to incur more debt. Before you make the leap to going off-grid, you should do your best to pay off all of your debts. Start small and get rid of your smallest debts first then work your way into the larger debts. Take whatever extra money that you earn from selling the things you are decluttering and put that towards your debts.

Saving on food

Food is another very large expense that people can easily save money on. Meal planning is a great option for being very conscious about what you are buying and how much you are spending. If your goal is to become self-sustainable with your food, this is also a great way to start saving money. You can start by purchasing food from a local farmer or you can start a small garden. Purchasing generic foods and other items can save a lot of money as well, unless of course, you have coupons that make brand name items cheaper.

If you are not super great at meal planning, then it would be wise to keep some frugal essentials on hand to make quick and cheap meals. These frugal pantry staples can include things like:

- Eggs
- Chicken, beef, and vegetable broths
- Beans, legumes, and grains
- Baking essentials like flour, sugar, baking powder, yeast, etc
- Citrus fruits (lemons)
- Potatoes, onions, carrots
- Peanut butter
- Oats and other grains
- Creamed soups
- Spices and herbs

- ☒ Pasta and rice
- ☒ Chicken breasts and ground meat
- ☒ Oils
- ☒ Frozen vegetables
- ☒ Tortillas
- ☒ Cheeses

With these frugal pantry staples, you can make just about anything. Many of these items you can freeze, can, and or prepare ahead of time to save you both time and money on your food bill.

Saving on little expenses

Often times many people are hanging on to subscriptions that they hardly ever use and are wasting their money on. Take a look at some of the subscriptions that you are currently paying for, such as a gym membership, cable, subscription boxes, and so on. Think about all those "little" expenses that add up every month that you could do without.

These little expenses can also include those impulse buys at the grocery store or gas station or even going and getting coffee at a cafe instead of making your own. One of the ways that you can really determine where your money is going is to keep a spending journal. Much like a checkbook registry, write down every little expense you are incurring for a few weeks to a month. You might be really amazed as to how much you are spending on items or services that you don't actually need.

Make saving a no brainer

If your goal is to build up a savings (which you should be working towards), you can do so automatically without ever having to think about it. If you get your salary or paycheck direct deposited, have an automatic withdrawal right from your check into your savings. I've talked about a couple of different ways to make some extra money when you are downsizing, such as selling your items to make a profit. Take that profit and any other "extra" money that you get (tax returns, inheritance, etc) and stick that right into your savings account.

You can also use apps and financial services that round up and save for you. For example, if you are going grocery shopping and your total is $58.32, then your bank or app would round up to the nearest whole dollar amount and put the rest into your savings. This is a great, no-brainer way to stockpile money into your savings without having to think about it. You can also use this rounding-up method to start investing as well, which is another great way to save for retirement.

Save on utilities

Considering when you are living off-grid you need to be more aware of your energy and water use, why not start now? Here are some ways that you can save on your utility bills now while also developing habits that will help you save energy and money while living off-grid:

- ☒ Take shorter, cooler showers

- ☒ Switch out your light bulbs for energy-efficient ones

- ☒ Wear clothes more than once and cut down on laundry

- ☒ Use a programmable thermostat

- ☒ Not cranking up the hot or cold air

- ☒ Winterize your windows during the cold months (or invest in better ones)

- ☒ Unplugging appliances when you are not actively using them

- ☒ Use low-flow water fixtures for your sinks, showers, and toilets

- ☒ Use cold or warm water when washing your clothes (not hot)

- ☒ Use smart power strips

Developing these habits and changes now can all help to get you in the mindset of living off-grid and saving energy.

Rent or borrow-don't buy

One thing that people underestimate is the friendliness of neighbors and friends. If you have to buy an appliance or something only to use it once or twice, try to borrow or rent one instead. Think about the big (expensive) stand mixer you purchased only to make macaroons once that now sits in your cupboard.

I'm am sure that you know someone you can borrow or rent items from in order to avoid having to buy them and waste money on things you hardly use, not to mention such things just take up more space. If you need to use larger items, like scaffolding to remodel, you can also rent such larger and more difficult to find items from national hardware stores.

Also, check at your local library to see what kinds of items they have for rent, you might be surprised. I have seen local libraries rent out kilowatt monitors to check how much wattage your home electrical appliances use. Not something that you would necessarily need to buy, but would be great to help figure out how to cut down on electricity costs.

Be a cheapskate

My friends call me a cheapskate, but I certainly don't mind.

Being a cheapskate has allowed me to live the life of my dreams. Don't be afraid to ask about any available discounts, you never know what is available until you ask, you can do this if you go out to eat or even from your cell phone provider. Before you transition to living off the grid, don't be afraid to call your electric company to see if there is any way that you can lower your bill. Many electric companies offer a budget plan where they put on you on a set, budgeted amount for six months at a time. This is very helpful when you are trying to budget your money.

If you are someone who enjoys going out to eat with friends and other entertainment type activities, don't be ashamed of being a cheapskate here also. Ask your server if there are any specials or discounts available. Check out local coupon apps before going out to get deals on items and experiences. I have saved a TON of money by doing this, it just takes a little planning ahead sometimes, but it is totally worth it to save some cash.

Do it yourself

I also do my best to avoid making a purchase when I can potentially DIY the item. Before you call a contractor to help you with any home remodel, watch some YouTube videos and Google "how to…" and try your own hand at the project.

You can potentially DIY just about anything for your house, camper, or RV. If there is something you want to do but aren't very skilled at it, ask around to people you know that might be able to help. You can either pay them a lower labor cost or trade services with them. Many people are still open to barter; don't be afraid to ask.

There are hundreds and thousands of ways to save more money every month, this list doesn't even scratch the surface. When you just start out with trying to save money it can be appealing to try and do everything at once, I get it. However, don't overwhelm yourself to the point where you feel like giving up. Work on one area at a time and incorporate more ways to save as you develop better and better habits.

Chapter Summary

Going off-grid also requires some downsizing and embracing minimalism. Getting rid of things that you don't need or serve no purpose is going to bring you such a sense of joy and satisfaction. Downsizing will also help make your transition to off-grid living so much easier. Most people have way more than they actually need. While you might not be transitioning into a tiny home, downsizing your belongings will help you to minimize distractions and let you focus on more important things in your life.

Some of the things that you can focus on downsizing include clothes, tech items, appliances, and trinkets. You really only need enough clothes to last you about a week with some special occasion items. Creating a capsule wardrobe with key items to mix and match will not only cut down on the space you need for your clothes but will also help save on doing laundry.

Cut down on your tech gadgets to the bare minimum. Also cut down on your kitchen appliances and keep or invest in ones that do multiple things rather than owning multiple appliances that only each serve one specific purpose. Opt for the most energy-efficient appliances as well.

When it comes to family heirlooms and trinkets, create a photo album or scrapbook with pictures of larger items rather than keeping the items themselves. See if other family members want to take the heirlooms. You are not trying to get rid of the memory, just the physical item.

There are many benefits to decluttering your home including physically, mentally, with your interpersonal relationships, finances, health, and overall well being. I am not suggesting that you get rid of all your worldly possessions and move into a tiny house, although that is a possibility. Minimalism is all about living a meaningful life without clutter to focus on your health and personal development.

Don't just start going through your house willy nilly and tossing things out. Take some time to think about your *why*. Why you want to get rid of things and what you are hoping to accomplish. Partake in a lifestyle audit and connect your vision of your ideal life with reality but make sure you are being honest with yourself.

Decluttering isn't just about minimizing your physical items, it also means your digital life as well. Unsubscribe to the millions of emails that you never read, organize your digital files and close out your dozens of computer tabs. Try to unplug for certain periods of time as well and enjoy time without technology.

Getting your finances in order is important whether you are going to live off the grid or not. You can't be successful in going off-grid if you don't have your finances in order. Poor money habits will follow you no matter where you go. You shouldn't have to worry about incurring more debt in achieving your off-grid lifestyle. Put any extra money you earn into paying off your debt or into your savings to help save for your off-grid transition.

Save on food by meal planning, shopping locally, and keeping frugal pantry staples on hand. Cut back on all the little expenses that you can by avoiding impulse buys and tracking what you are spending your money on. Set up an automatic deposit into your savings account or use an app or banking service that roundups your purchases and saves or invests the extra automatically.

Save on utilities by making lifestyle adjustments and swapping out appliances for energy-efficient ones. Rent or borrow items that you will only use a few times from friends, family, libraries, or hardware stores. Don't be afraid to be a cheapskate and ask for discounts and find coupons and ways to save where you can. Wherever possible, try and do it yourself (as long as you can do it safely) to save some extra money.

In the next chapter, we are going to cover the different types of off-grid dwellings, how and where to find your ideal property (whether to build new or bring your home along with you), and how to put together your grand plan for going off-grid.

CHAPTER THREE:
Off-Grid Property, What Is Right For You?

L IVING OFF THE grid is a big commitment. You have to determine what type of off-grid living is right for you, which can include a lot of research.

In this chapter, we are going to cover the different types of off-grid homes, how to figure out where to buy a property or land, and formulating your plan for off-grid living.

The Different Types of Off-Grid Homes

In the first chapter, we covered the three main types of off-grid living: roughing it, half-on/ half-off, and modern off-grid living. In addition to the types of off-grid living, there are also several types of off-grid style homes. This can include anything from a huge farm to an RV used to travel the world.

Tiny homes

Tiny homes have become increasingly popular. While tiny homes can be on the grid, there are many that are off-grid. Tiny homes appeal to many as there are many aspects that can be built by the owner. It also forces minimalism as there isn't enough room to keep extra stuff you don't need.

Tiny homes are generally solar powered but can also be wind-powered. Tiny homes can also be a very affordable option to traditionally larger homes as tiny homes usually cost only a few thousand dollars to build (depending, of course, on how big the home is and what is included). Tiny homes are also a great way to reduce your ecological footprint as well as save a ton of money. Living in a tiny home frees up your time for other things like personal development and creative pursuits as you don't have to worry about working so hard to pay for a mortgage or maintaining a much larger house.

Tiny homes promote sustainability and self-sufficiency. Many people build their own tiny homes which means they have a greater understanding of how their homes work and how they can make them work more efficiently. Tiny homes can also be placed on very small parcels of land or much larger properties. They can also be stationary or mobile. Tiny homes can also be rural or urban.

An obvious downside to living in a tiny house is the lack of space. While this can force you to spend more time outside (when the weather is nice), they aren't for everyone. Tiny homes also are not great for larger families and work better for single people, couples, or a maximum of about three people. There can also be a lack of privacy as you are living in very close quarters with one or two other people.

Homestead

Homesteading is pretty much what everyone did before moving into the cities. In order to be a successful homesteader, it is going to require some planning and preparation. Homesteading is generally a larger, stationary home placed on a larger parcel of land. It is characterized by striving for a self-sustaining lifestyle.

Homesteading occurs on a rural property where the owner is free from all of the hustle and bustle of noisy city life. Homesteading is a great option for raising a family, especially a larger one, and you generally don't have to worry about neighbors being too close.

Homesteading focuses a lot on being self-sustainable. Homesteaders tend to grow a lot of their own food, raise their own animals, and often make their own natural products. Many homesteaders also earn a living from the food they grow, animals they raise, or products they make.

Homesteading also has the potential to save a lot of money. When you grow your own food, you are just paying for seeds and can drastically cut down on your grocery bill. When you combine homesteading with off-grid living you can save a significant amount on bills such as water and electricity as well.

As with any type of living situation, there are also a few downsides to homesteading. It can be expensive to get started. It generally requires a larger investment in a home and land. In addition, if you have to convert parts of the property to off-grid, solar panels and septic tanks can be pricey to install initially.

If you live out in the boondocks on your homestead, you don't have the luxury of running to the corner store when you need something. It can also be difficult to get internet and phone service in more rural areas. This can lead to a rather large internet and phone bill depending on what area you live in. However, you can still have a homestead and be pretty close to neighboring towns and have decent internet and phone access.

Cabin

Cabins are great for those that would rather have peace and quiet in the woods. Cabins can be wired and include indoor plumbing or "dry cabins" like I mentioned earlier in the roughing it section. You can easily install solar panels for electric and gravity pumps for plumbing. Although you might need to spend some time chopping up firewood if you are taking the wood-burning heat route.

Living in a cabin is like a cross between homesteading and tiny home living. The cabin itself can be any size. It can be in a rural area or a more urban area. It can be fully wired and include plumbing while still being off-grid or totally roughing it style.

The main characteristic of a cabin is the main material used to build the house, which is usually logs. Some of the downsides of owning a log cabin include little to no room for insulation, which means it can get colder during the winter months and need more wood to burn for heat. Let's not forget about those pesky bugs and insects that feed on wood. Cabins can also be complicated to wire with electricity because you don't want to damage those beautiful logs. Log cabins, depending on the size, of course, can be very expensive to build.

Other than the immense beauty of log homes, they are "greener" homes. They offer a wonderfully cozy, warm, and relaxed feeling with all the natural woodwork. If the logs are caulked properly, they are much more energy-efficient than standard homes. Also, log walls offer natural sound insulation. You can also install drywall over the logs to create a normal looking wall that you can paint or make installation of insulation for temperature control and wiring for electricity easier.

Earth homes

An earth home is one that is covered with earth or built into the earth. While this is probably the least common type of home among off-gridders, it is certainly an option to consider. Earth homes are great for energy conservation where you don't have to worry about running air conditioning even in warmer climates. They also hold heat better in the cooler months as well. Earth homes tend to be more secure than traditional homes, which can give the owner greater peace of mind. They also offer greater protection from the outdoor elements.

One of the biggest disadvantages of living in an earth home is the lack of windows, which means less sunlight. However, you can install skylights to try and let in more light in certain areas of your home. You should also be aware that earth homes have a higher susceptibility to water problems after heavy rains. Earth homes require much more waterproofing than traditional homes. Earth homes should have two or more exits in case of a fire to ensure the safety of the inhabitants.

RVing

RV living can include living in an RV, mobile camper, or even a converted van. RV and van living has become increasingly popular. Many people are ditching their traditional living quarters for the full-time RV lifestyle. People are also building businesses to sustain their RV living through writing and making videos about their RV lifestyles.

One of the biggest appeals to full-time RV living is the freedom of being able to go where you want when you want. There is a level of freedom that you can achieve with living full-time in an RV that you can't with any other type of off-grid living (except maybe a mobile tiny home).

You never have to worry about annoying neighbors or mowing your lawn. You can develop a closer relationship with whomever you are living with (or yourself) as you are in such close quarters. You also don't have to worry about accumulating junk as you won't have any room for extra stuff you don't need.

RV living can also come with many uncertainties, like not always having access to hot water. RV water heaters can take some time to heat up to the correct temperature, so plan accordingly when you want a hot shower. If you don't have a composting toilet, which I highly recommend, then you have to worry about emptying your black tank. Let me tell you, this is not a pleasant experience!

Living in an RV can also lend itself to being rather buggy. Considering most RVs can never be completely sealed, bugs find their way into tiny crevasses. However, you can always spray your RV with some bug repellant to try and prevent too many bugs from getting in.

Most RVs are going to require a bit of renovation if you are going to make it your full-time home. Admittedly, RVs and campers are not very stylish. But with some interior design skills, you can make a really awesome looking RV that fits your style.

While the initial purchase of an RV can be pricey, the continued cost of RV living is fairly minimal. Electric, heat, insurance, and internet for RVs are generally very affordable. You can experience higher costs when parking your RV in certain national, state and RV parks.

Houseboat

Another form of off-grid living that is a little less conventional is living in a houseboat. This is a great option for those that love the water. While houseboats come in many sizes, generally you are looking at about 400 to 500 square feet of living space, which are boats 40-60 feet in length. There are at least eight different types of houseboats you can live in, we won't get into each one of those here, but just know that if you decide to go with the houseboat option, you are going to have more research to do.

Rather than paying any kind of property tax, you are going to need to pay a vessel registration fee. Just as with RV living, people choose to live on houseboats for the freedom it offers, not to mention some amazing views.

Some of the costs associated with living on a boat are marina fees, registration, insurance, having the sewage tank pumped, and other normal bills such as electric and internet. There is certainly a lot less work to do outside of your home than with a traditional home, other than washing your house off.

One disadvantage of owning a houseboat and attempting to travel is that unlike the RV lifestyle, you can't exactly tow your car behind your houseboat. If you are traveling you are probably going to have to rent a vehicle once you dock in your new location. Or, if the weather is nice enough, you can always bring a bike along.

With any type of off-grid home, there tends to be more physical labor involved, such as hauling water, emptying a compost toilet, or other physical challenges. There can also be some challenges that come with government regulations and codes. Generally speaking, the closer you are to civilization, cities, towns, etc, the more rules and regulations you are going to have to work through. You will also have to figure out if you are required to pay taxes on your property or land.

Deciding Where To Buy Property Or Land

Picking where you are going to start your off-grid living is just as important as picking which type of home you are going to live in. The land itself is not that difficult to find, there is land everywhere all over the world. Land is available in all different types of areas, all different sizes, and prices. While you might have some ideal aspects already in mind, there are a couple of key factors to consider when looking for your perfect off-grid parcel of land.

You should have easy access to water. We as humans need clean water to survive. While this might sound obvious, there are many places in the country that don't have easy access to water and they have to haul it many miles. This is probably not something you are going to want to do. Having to haul water from a faraway source is not a sustainable way to live. While you don't necessarily need to be living on a lake, you should look for land in which you have access to a clean and natural water source, such as a lake, river, stream, natural spring, or well.

While access to natural building materials is not necessary, it can be extremely helpful. The greater access you have to trees provides you with lumber for building your home or other projects that you might need. You can also use lumber to build things to sell for a profit to help sustain your off-grid living. Other natural materials such as stone, rocks, clay, and mud are also great building resources. Having access to natural building materials also saves you a lot of money in the long run as they are sustainable and readily available.

You also have to consider the practicality of the land you would like to build on. While you might have found the most beautiful property with amazing sunsets, if it comes with too many building codes or restrictions then it might not be worth it.

Location is also very important. With off-grid living becoming more popular, there are certain US states that promote off-grid living, such as Colorado, Oklahoma, Alaska, Wyoming, Arkansas, and Missouri. You should consider energy generation and climate when choosing your location. While no two people are going to have the same ideal for their locations, consider the amount of sun you want to get, as well as wind, snow, rain, and humidity. While some people enjoy full sun, others prefer snow and cold.

If you are going to be off-grid (which is the point here) you are going to need access to sun and wind to create power for yourself. You can do some research to determine which locations are best for you to self-generate power in the places you are interested in living.

Additional important aspects to consider when determining your off-grid home's location are the zoning, building codes, ordinances, covenants, and other restrictions. It doesn't really matter where or how hard you are looking, there are always going to be some kind of restrictions, zoning, or building ordinances. If you are looking to avoid zoning restrictions and regulations, it is best to stay away from larger cities. This is where your research is going to come in handy, so make sure that you are doing your research in advance before you pack up all your belongings and head off to your ideal location. It is best to choose a property in which you have minimal restrictions.

Your property should have easy access to where you are going to place your home on that property and to reliable roads. Whether this access is a paved road or driveway or some other type of way to get back and forth to your home, it is critical you know and ensure access before buying the property. While you might find the most beautiful piece of property, if you can't access it, or build a way to access it, then it is going to be pointless to try to live there.

Of course, don't forget about the affordability of

the piece of land that you want. It is entirely up to you whether or not you want to take out a loan for your perfect piece of property. I, personally, prefer to go totally off-grid and not be tied to a bank or any other financial institution. Many people do not have the means (aka credit score) to get a loan from a traditional bank. Part of living off of the grid is to be debt-free and cut ties from traditional institutions. You can do this by buying land directly from the landowner. When you can buy directly from the landowner you can generally pay off your land faster as it will have a lower monthly payment and a lower interest rate. You can either negotiate with the landowner yourself or use a buyer's agent, which is similar to a real estate agent.

The land that you buy is what is going to allow you to complete your off-grid lifestyle. Finding the perfect property for your off-grid lifestyle is going to take time. It's going to take research. It's going to take some trial and error. It's going to be frustrating at times (or a lot of times), but it is worth it.

Formulating Your Grand Plan

If you are going to be doing your off-grid lifestyle with a partner, your grand plan needs to start with a conversation. Whether or not you are going to live with someone else when you go off-grid, you need to determine your *why*. Why do you want to - or feel the need to - pursue the off-grid lifestyle? Is it your love of nature? Your love of travel? Your longing to rid yourself of traditional institutions? Your desire to save a lot of money over your lifetime? The ability to live life on your own terms? Or all of the above?

Once you have determined your why, you can start to scope out locations. This is probably going to take you some time, so don't be afraid of starting this process early. You might be able to find your ideal location within weeks or it could take you years. Remember the exercise that I told you I did at the beginning of the book, the visualization of my ideal day? I want you to do that exercise now. What does your ideal piece of land look like? What do your daily activities look like? What does your home look like? What do your finances look like? How do you feel, physically and emotionally? What is your work lifelike, and so on?

Also, consider some of the more technical aspects such as building codes, water, and energy systems, building materials, and so forth.

Once you have the main aspects of your physical space worked out, start doing your research! Go online and search to see which areas fit your criteria. Read blogs and watch videos from others that are already living the lifestyle you want to live. If there is a certain area that you keep coming back to, then go and visit it if possible. Spend some time as close to your ideal location as you can. Visit the location in all four seasons to see if the weather conditions are something you can handle, especially if you are going for a kind of dwelling that is going to be affected by the elements.

Find a realtor or broker's agent that is familiar

with working with individuals that are looking to go off-grid. Working with someone that has experience in this area will help to lessen your stress in finding your perfect property.

Once you have determined the best type of property for you, you can also work on finding the best dwelling for you as well. It is entirely your personal preference - whether or not you are purchasing land with a home, purchasing the land and putting a home on it, not purchasing land and using a home that you can move - it is all up to you. Whatever your choice, you need to work on downsizing your current home and work on the other things we discussed in the previous chapter.

However you put together your grand plan you should keep all of your ideas and plans in one central place. Start a notebook, a scrapbook, a spreadsheet - whatever works best for you. While I could give you a step by step plan as to what you need to do, making this big of a life transition is very personal. You need to decide what is best for you and your family.

Chapter Summary

We have determined by now that going off-grid is a very big commitment. It requires a lot of research to determine which type of dwelling is best for you and your situation, what type of property will work best for you, and how best to begin formulating your grand plan.

The various types of off-grid homes include tiny

homes, homesteads, cabins, earth homes, RVs, and houseboats. There are pros and cons to each of these types of dwellings including fees, regulations, sizing, sanitation, mobility, and so forth.

Determining what type of property is best for you also requires a lot of research and time. While there are many options for land available you should ensure that you have easy access to fresh water, the land is practical to build on. The land should also be in your preferred climate, the zoning and regulation should not be too strict. The land should be accessible to and from reliable roads and, ideally, you have the flexibility to finance a piece of land with the landowner.

When it comes to formulating your grand plan, before doing anything else, you should determine your why. Why do you want to live off-grid? Imagine your ideal day and your ideal life. What about that day makes living off-grid ideal for you? Visualize your ideal life living off the grid and keep track of all of your research in a notebook or spreadsheet.

In the next chapter, we are going to cover all things related to water use and consumption in relation to off-grid living.

CHAPTER FOUR:
Everything You Need To Know About Water

W HAT DO HUMANS need to survive?
One of the biggest aspects of survival is clean water. While living in the city you might take clean, running water for granted, living off-grid is an entirely different experience when it comes to how you manage your water usage.

In this chapter, I will cover how to find and source water from natural sources, what is necessary to install a water well, the various kinds of water storage systems, what a water pressure tank is and how to use one and the different kinds of water filtration and purification systems available for different types of dwellings.

Natural, Reliable Water Sources

In the previous chapter, I mentioned finding a property in which you had easy access to clean and natural water. If you can find a property that has a stream, river, lake, well, or a natural spring, congratulations, you just made one part of off-grid living a whole lot easier. With these types of water access, you should never have to worry about running out of fresh, clean water. While these forms of freshwater are pretty straight forward, there are other ways to gather and collect natural water that you might not have considered, such as rainwater harvesting or water cisterns.

If you don't already have access to a natural pond or river, you can make a manmade pond, if you have a big enough lot. All of the aforementioned natural (or manmade) water sources can be used to water livestock, water crops, and bathe. After purification, water from such sources can also be used for drinking and cooking.

If you have a stream or river, you can utilize that source for hydropower as well as for drinking and bathing. You can easily rig up a pump into the stream to provide water directly into your dwelling. You should consider the terrain when installing a pump, as it is going to take a stronger pump to move water from a stream or river uphill to your property.

Many people that live off-grid use the rainwater collection method. If you are in an area that gets a lot, or a normal amount of rainfall, rainwater collection is a great option. You can collect rainwater using large collection barrels and filter/purify the water for consumption. Generally, rain barrels are connected to gutters on the dwelling using pipes. Just be sure to check your local ordinances to ensure that you are not doing anything illegal. Yes, collecting rainwater in some areas is illegal, silly I know.

Installing A Water Well

If you do not have access to fresh water via a stream, river, lank, pond, or spring, you might need to drill your own well. While wells are a great option, especially if you are on lower ground closer to a water table, they can be rather expensive and there is no guarantee with drilling a well that you will actually get access to water. It requires research to make an informed decision about drilling a well on a given property.

Wells are great for providing a clean and consistent source of chemical-free water. If you want to use a well as your water source and need to drill one, it is best to check with your local geological office before breaking ground. There is a lot more that goes into digging a well then just digging a hole in the ground and hoping for the best (FYI...NEVER do that!) Contact a professional well-driller to ensure that you are drilling in the correct spot and the soil conditions are ideal for a well.

When drilling a well, you need to determine if it is going to be drilled or driven. This all depends on the depth that the water is underground and the nature of the soil. The depth of the water underground can also vary drastically from region to region. Underground water can be a few feet below the surface or hundreds of feet below the surface and through porous sand and silt.

Make sure to contact your local utility company to ensure that there are not any service lines on your property that would potentially be damaged if you start digging. You also need to determine if there are any old underground cisterns, sewer lines, and septic systems on the land. You can inquire with your local building code to determine if any permits are needed.

Water Storage Systems

If you are in a situation where you have to haul water on occasion, having an efficient water storage system is imperative. This can be done effectively with a cistern or water hauling tank. If you don't have access to a freshwater source, then you will likely have to have water hauled to your homestead or dwelling. While this isn't the most economical or sustainable option, sometimes it might be the only option. You can also use a water storage system as a backup in case of an emergency. If you are collecting rainwater as a source of water, being able to store it is very important.

Water storage systems can be kept above ground or below ground. The type of storage system that you choose will depend on the climate that you are living in. If you are living in a warmer climate that does not go below freezing then an above-ground storage system will often work fine. If you are living in colder climates, a below groundwater storage tank is a better option. They can be placed low enough into the ground to prevent freezing of the water and prevent the tank from cracking and becoming damaged.

Underground tanks also prevent contamination of the water. While underground tanks are more expensive, they are necessary for colder climates. Underground tanks also require a water pump to extract the water out of the cistern.

Tanks that are above ground are generally considered water hauling tanks. They are smaller than below ground tanks and are generally portable to allow for hauling back and forth from the water source to the dwelling.

Water Pressure Tanks

Those living in the city are used to having pressurized water without having to think about it. You can turn on the shower and have a nice stream of water pressure to rinse yourself with without ever having to think about how the water is being pressurized. If your property already has a well, it is likely that it already has an electric pump installed in which it will continue to have pressurized water whenever you want it.

A water pressure tank essentially adds energy to the water and pushes or pulls it to move it in one direction or another. When water is pushed, it creates pressure.

Having a water pressure tank allows you to have pressurized water for more than a couple of seconds by creating pressure in stored water.

You first have your water source, then your pump to get the water to where it needs to go. In this case, when you have a pressure tank, the water is pumped into the water tank. The water from the pressure tank is then expelled into various faucets and fixtures.

You could take out the pressure tank and run the pump 24/7, but that presents other issues. Running an electric well pump 24/7 will drastically eat at your energy expenditure. Installing a water pressure tank helps to keep the water pressurized when the pump is not actually running. Once the pressure in the tank drops below a certain amount the pump will turn back on and start to pressurize the water again.

You may not need a very large water pressure tank if you have a small property and a small home, generally larger homesteads require larger pressure tanks. The larger the pressure tank is the less the water pump has to work. The less the water pump has to turn off and on the less power, it also uses. If you aren't fully off-grid and still hooked up to a power company having a larger pressure tank allows you to have access to water on demand in an emergency. If you are not connected to the electric grid, this generally is not a concern as the water pump can also be run on a generator.

Water Filtration And Purification

With any type of water collection, you should filter and purify your water to ensure that it is safe for human consumption. Filtering your water is a very safe and effective option for making sure your water is safe to drink. There are commercial filters that can process up to 15 or more gallons of water per day. These filters are often made from carbon and charcoal and are able to remove harmful substances such as pathogens, lead, mercury, arsenic, and other potentially harmful chemicals.

If you are trying to filter water within your whole house, it is suggested to install a reverse osmosis system to filter the water coming in and out of your house. Using a reverse osmosis system, you can get great tasting water that is extremely clean and good for you. Reverse osmosis systems are pretty low maintenance and are fairly cost-effective in comparison to having something like a water delivery service. There is a bit more research that goes into choosing the best reverse osmosis system for your home and going off-grid as often reverse osmosis systems require higher water pressure to work properly.

You can also purify water by boiling it, straining it through cheesecloth, making a DIY activated charcoal filter, and other types of makeshift filters in order to make your water safe to drink. While commercial water filters can be pricey, but well worth it, there are many ways to make a DIY water filter using objects found in your home. Also, boiling water does not remove impurities so boiling alone is not effective, you need to take the second step of straining it as well.

While not the best option, you can also use chlorine to purify water, if you don't have any other options for clean drinking water available. Chlorine also doesn't leave the best aftertaste, it's like drinking pool water. However, if you are in a pinch, keeping some chlorine tabs on hand is always wise. Just make sure to let the water sit for a bit before chugging it down to avoid ingesting other additional chemicals.

Chapter Summary

We all need water to survive and getting clean water to your property can be a challenge for many. If at all possible, source your water from a natural source that is located on your property, such as a stream, river, pond, spring, or well. Other ways of getting natural water include water collection via rainwater harvesting and above or below ground cisterns.

When planning out your water source you must also consider your water needs. Do you have livestock to water? How big are the crops that you are planning on planting? Are you going to have to pump uphill to your property or house?

One of the main advantages of having a larger natural water source on your property, such as a pond or river, is that you can also use that for hydropower. In addition to whatever type of water source you will use, many people living off-grid also choose to collect rainwater to have an additional emergency source of water.

If you do not have access to natural water sources above-ground on your property you may want to consider installing a well. While this can be a more expensive option it offers a great consistent source of fresh water. If you decide to drill for a well, make sure that you are contacting your local geological office before you begin digging to ensure the safety of not hitting any underground lines.

If you need to haul water to your property either consistently or on occasion, you will need to have an effective water storage system in place. Depending on the temperature during the winter months you can either use an above ground or below groundwater storage system. If your property does not already include a water pump and water pressure tank, and if you want to shower with some actual water pressure, then these are additional expenses to consider.

Again, depending on where you are sourcing your water from you also need to consider how you plan to filter and purify your water to make it safe for drinking. This can be done using a commercial water filtration system such as a reverse osmosis system or a DIY system. You can also purify your water by boiling it and straining it or, as a last resort, by adding chlorine.

In the next chapter, we are going to cover what to do with your water once it is no longer safe for drinking, otherwise known as wastewater.

CHAPTER FIVE:
Handling Waste On Your Homestead: Sewage And Septic Systems

NOW THAT WE have covered everything you need to know about how to get water to your property and filtered so that it is safe for human consumption, let's talk about what happens to that water when it is no longer safe. Wastewater is not a hot topic that you will see many others talking about; however, it is a very important topic that should not be ignored.

In this chapter, we are going to discuss the standard kinds of holding tanks, how a pressure distribution septic system works, and, my favorite, composting toilets. Because, as we all know, what goes in must come out...and it has to go somewhere.

Standard Holding Tanks

While there are some people out there who don't care about the environment or the disposal of their... disposal, I am going to bet that you don't want to add anything else to the Earth that is going to harm it. This is why, although not a pretty subject, the topic of treatment and management of wastewater, or black water, is essential and absolutely necessary in your education about off-grid living.

Installing a septic tank is an affordable solution for many people going off-grid. A standard holding tank is used to hold greywater, or water that is used to do your laundry, wash your hands with and shower with. While it's not likely that you are going to drink that water, it can be used for other things in your home, such as flushing waste in your toilet.

Treated greywater can be used to water plants that are both food-producing and non-food producing. You can also use water that you have washed your hands with to do laundry with. Rather than wasting water on one use, try and use it multiple times to conserve the water that you do have.

Any water that you use that then is deemed greywater can be diverted into a separate holding tank which can then be connected to your toilet or treated for other household uses. Being able to reuse your greywater is a great way of reducing your dependence on freshwater, which can be especially helpful when you are hauling water and don't have access to an unlimited water supply.

Depending on the size of your family, how much water you use, and how much greywater you generate and re-use, your septic tank should be serviced every few years. A general rule of thumb for septic tank servicing is about three to six years. This requires a professional septic pumping company to come in and pump out the tank. Standard holding tanks and septic tanks are gravity fed and do not require an additional pump to move the water from one spot to another. If that is necessary on your property, that will require a pressure distribution septic system.

Pressure Distribution Septic System

If there is not enough gravity to move the wastewater from your home to your septic system, you will require a pressure distribution septic system. Pressure distribution septic tanks have several advantages. With traditional septic tanks, the water is drained into the septic tank via gravity. The blackwater can then be partially filtered there and then continue to flow downwards into a series of pipes and eventually into a leach field. A leach field is used in addition to a septic tank to get rid of impurities and pollutants in the wastewater before it leaves the septic tank. An entire septic system is made up of a septic tank, leach field, and any piping that goes along with the entire system.

Secondly, with a gravity-fed system, the distribution

of wastewater is localized and stays in a small handful of locations. As gravity controls the flow of water, where it goes, and how quickly it gets there, this can lead to issues with soil flooding, contamination of the ground-water, and oversaturation of the absorption area.

A pressure distribution septic system solves these issues by taking dependence on gravity out of the equation. A pressure distribution septic system does not replace any part of the septic system, but rather adds to it to make it more efficient. If the leach field is located uphill from the septic tank, the pressure systems help to push the water where it needs to go.

The pressure distribution system includes a septic tank that works to separate solids from oils from the remainder of the wastewater. Once solids and oils have been separated, the remaining wastewater flows into a separate tank known as a dosing tank. The water is passed through a screen which removes any remaining solid waste. The second tank, the dosing tank, then pumps the wastewater into the leach field. The remaining water that flows through the leach field is distributed through holes in the pipes and into the soil for disposal and treatment. Unlike a gravity-fed septic tank, the dosing tank only allows a specific amount of wastewater to flow into the leach field to prevent flooding and contamination.

Composting Toilets

Composting toilets are great! I think every house, homestead, RV, cabin, and even apartment should have one (or two). Composting toilets can range from a bucket with some sawdust to rather elaborate (and expensive) composting toilets. The basic premise of a composting toilet is that the solids and liquids are separated and disposed of in eco-friendly ways.

One of the biggest benefits of composting toilets is that they don't use water. While there are many "low flow" toilets on the market that decrease water usage, on average it takes five to seven gallons to flush a toilet. Even the low flow toilets use almost one and a half gallons of water. Think about that for a minute. If you are flushing the toilet multiple times per day and there is more than one person in your household, that adds up to a lot of water. However, with composting toilets, the elimination of water usage saves a lot of money while also extending the life of your septic system, which again, saves you money.

The second big advantage of composting toilets, is that the waste that is produced can be used as compost, hence the name: composting toilet. Considering the waste decomposes naturally, it can be used in gardens and is free of pathogens and viruses when it is completely decomposed.

Preparing and dumping the waste from your compost toilet is not difficult at all. Grab a pair of gloves and remove the top part of the toilet. You can then use a composting bag to put the compost waste into. First, you remove the liquid waste bucket, then dump all of the compost material into the compost bag. You can then take the composting bag with the compost waste in it and dispose of it in the garbage or add it to a larger composting pile. Then just refill the part of the toilet where the solids go with more soil.

When disposing of the liquids from the tank you can dump them directly into a sewer, your gray water tank, or even directly into the ground. Depending on your living situation dumping on the ground may be illegal in some areas so just make sure you are checking (and obeying) your local ordinances.

Chapter Summary

While many people living in the city don't give much thought to their waste disposal, it is a very important topic to consider when going off-grid.

If your septic system is going to be located at a lower level than your dwelling, then a standard holding tank should do just fine. Standard holding tanks will hold and treat black wastewater. Greywater can then be diverted into a separate holding tank and be connected to a toilet used for flushing waste or used on other household activities such as watering plants. Standard septic tanks need to be serviced and pumped every few years by a professional septic pumping company.

If there is not enough gravity to move your waste-water into your septic tank system, then a pressure distribution septic tank is suggested. A pressure distribution septic tank helps to prevent flooding and contamination of wastewater in the leach field often associated with traditional gravity-fed septic systems.

Another great way to conserve water is to use composting toilets in your dwelling. These can be used in standard homes, RVs, cabins, and just about any other off-grid home (or on-grid home, for that matter). Using a composting toilet can help to save an immense amount of water and is especially helpful if you do not have access to vast amounts of freshwater from a natural source.

Composting toilets are also easy to install and the waste is also easy to dispose of. The solids from the composting bin within the toilet can be used in a larger composting pile and also used for gardening or thrown directly in the trash without ill effects on the environment.

In the next chapter, we will cover all of the various types of off-grid power systems including ways to reduce your energy consumption.

CHAPTER SIX:
All About Off-Grid Power

GOING OFF-GRID OFTEN refers to disconnecting from the local power utility company and providing your own power sources. How this is done can greatly depend on where your home will be located and what type of natural resources are readily available to you.

In this chapter, I am going to cover the various types of alternative power systems, how to use solar power, when it is best to use wind power, the pros and cons of geothermal power, how to effectively use propane and hydro-powered systems, what a powershed is, and ways to reduce your energy consumption.

Alternative Power Systems

Alternative power systems are relying on energy sources other than the use of fossil fuels. These alternative energy sources offer varying degrees of renewability and minimal environmental pollutants.

Homeowners are opting to go off-grid as a means to decrease their energy costs and not have to rely on utility companies for their sources of power.

While there are many types of alternative power systems, the most common include geothermal, solar, hydro, and wind. Depending on your location you can use one of these sources or combine them and use multiple sources together.

Solar Power

When it comes to residential alternative power sources, solar power is the most common and well known. Using solar power includes installing photo-voltaic solar panels, an inverter, and batteries. This is generally the best type of primary alternative power source to use as many areas have access to extended periods of sunlight. However, there are many places in the winter months that don't get a lot of sun, which would make it difficult to produce enough energy from solar panels in these areas.

Using solar power is a low-maintenance option but can cost a bit to get started with. Solar panels only provide energy when the sun is shining or slightly overcast. You can get started with a solar panel energy kit for as little as $5,000.

Solar energy is a great way to start exploring alter-native power systems, especially if you are choosing the half-on/half-off type of off-grid lifestyle. This allows you to draw energy from the solar panels during the day and use power from the grid when it is dark or overcast. Even if you are not drawing energy from the grid, one of the biggest advantages of staying connected to the grid is the ability to sell back your surplus energy to the power company (more on that in a minute).

As I said before, the solar panel system is made up of three components: the solar panels, the inverter, and the battery. The solar panels are what collect energy from the sun. When you are installing them you should pick an area on your property that gets the most sunlight, either on the roof of your home, garage, barn, or an open field.

There is also the option of installing a solar optimizer. While not required, it does offer some big advantages. The effectiveness of the solar panel system is determined by the weakest panel. This means that if one panel is dirty or partially shaded that this will bring down the efficiency of the rest of the solar panels. Installing a solar panel optimizer essentially separates the solar panels and optimizes their power individually. Therefore, if there is power loss from one panel, the entire system is not compromised. An optimizer also helps to increase the overall life of the solar panel system.

The power inverter is the next necessary component in the solar panel system. The main function of the inverter is to change the power from the sun into power you can use on everyday energy expenditures. When the sun's energy is collected by the solar panels it is called direct current, the inverter changes the direct current into alternating current. The alternating current is what is used to power your TV, your computer, and even your air conditioning. There are several different types of inverters and various factors that will determine which is the best for your property. For example, an off-grid converter is used if you are completely off-grid, whereas a battery backup inverter allows you to store energy and send it back to the grid.

A solar panel battery helps to store the energy that is produced by the solar panels for later use. Instead of sending your energy back to the grid, you can keep it stored in the battery for use on cloudy days or during the evening. These can also work as a short-term backup in case of a power outage from the grid (if you are still connected).

Selling Your Surplus Energy Back To The Grid

Selling your energy back to the grid doesn't mean that you will get a check every month from your utility company (although that would be awesome!)

When you are collecting solar energy and you have a surplus, this is known as net energy metering. Essentially you are storing energy in the grid for later use. When you have a surplus in energy it is stored on the grid as credits. When you need to pull energy from the grid, it uses up your credits rather than having to pay for it in the traditional sense. This is one major advantage of staying connected to the grid.

However, you have to check to make sure your state allows for net metering, as only about 41 currently do. In addition to getting energy credits from the grid, you can also sell solar energy to your neighbors using peer to peer energy trading.

There are also tax credits offered to individuals that are taking measures to make their homes more sustainable and energy-efficient. Most recently, the US federal government is offering a solar tax credit which allows both commercial and residential installers to deduct up to 30% of the cost of the solar energy system from your federal taxes. However, this can change from year to year so make sure that you are keeping up to date with the latest in solar energy tax advantages.

Wind Power

With using wind power you need to ensure that you get enough wind in your area to power a residential turbine. You can easily do this by contacting your local weather service and asking what the average wind speed is in the area. When you figure out the average wind speed, you can then calculate the estimated amount of energy that will be produced. Keep in mind though, the wind speed at a specific location can differ drastically than the average in the area due to location topography.

Residential wind turbines generally come in three sizes: 400-watt, 90-watt, and 10,000-wat. The 400-watt turbine has a four-foot diameter rotor and can be used to power a few appliances in your home. The 900-watt is a seven-foot turbine, which many people opt for as you don't need a ton of room to install it. Lastly, the 10,000-watt is a 23-foot turbine that is mounted on a tower that is 100 feet or taller. While you need a lot of room for this, it can generate enough power to power your entire home.

Wind power is great to use on its own or in addition to solar power or other alternative power sources. It can be stored in a battery or used directly in water pumping applications, such as to power your pressure distribution septic tank. Combining a wind-powered system, or hybrid system, is especially useful when you live in an area that doesn't get much sun in the winter or is often cloudy (if you are combining with a solar system that is).

It is also very affordable to get started with wind power, as a smaller turbine can cost less than $1,000. A hybrid solar and wind system is very common and these two complement each other well. While you won't get much solar energy in the winter or during bad weather, the wind is often increased during such times.

Wind power is much cleaner and sustainable as opposed to using a gas-powered generator. Furthermore, it only takes winds of five to eight miles per hour to generate power, which really is not a lot. You can even get a hybrid kit that has everything you need for both solar and wind power for your home, either completely off-grid or a grid tie-in kit. Wind systems are also extremely low maintenance.

Geothermal Power

Geothermal power draws heat out of the earth in order to power your home. Geothermal energy is sort of like solar energy in that the ground absorbs about 40% of the sun's energy into the first 500 feet of soil. By placing piping into the ground and circulating water through the piping it is then transferred into a unit within the home that looks similar to a furnace to convert into heat and hot water to use within the home.

Geothermal power, much like other forms of alternative energy sources, can be used in addition to other forms of energy. While it is one of the pricier options, it generally pays for itself within the first ten years of installation. With proper maintenance and care, it can last a good 40 to 50 years.

Hydro

Setting up a hydro system is great if you have a source of running water on your property, like a stream. With hydroelectricity, the energy is produced from the flow of water, which turns a turbine at the lower end of where the water flows. Hydro systems can be extremely cost-effective and the source of energy itself is easily harnessed.

For the same investment that you make into wind or solar panels, you can generate 10 to 100 times more power using a hydro system. If you have a good, reliable source of hydropower, it will produce energy for you

24/7. Which, in turn, provides you with off-grid energy for a very long time. Furthermore, because the energy is so consistent, you won't need to store the energy in batteries for later use.

The biggest downfall with hydro energy systems is that you actually need the proper on site conditions. No running water means no hydro system.

Propane

Propane is a cost-effective option for heating your home or for cooking. Not only is propane cost-effective, but it is also a clean-burning fuel that is available in abundance. Propane is stored in above-ground tanks that are periodically refilled and can be used for heating the home, hot water production, cooking, and many other purposes. Unlike wood-burning alternatives, you don't have to worry about spending hours chopping work or the potential fire hazards of wood-burning devices.

Propane, much like with other forms of alternative energy, can be used in combination with other energy sources. It costs about 30% less to install a propane water heater than it does a standard electric water heater. There are also tankless, propane water heaters that help to produce up to 60% fewer carbon emissions than traditional heaters. Tankless units also take less energy to heat up the water for use.

Propane is also a great source for running your appliances as well. You can use propane to power a stove or oven in addition to a battery to ignite the spark to get things started. There are even appliances that you can purchase that only require propane to run without the additional use of electricity. Some of the other types of appliances that you can run with off-grid propane are refrigerators, space heaters, grills, freezers, and clothes dryers. You can also invest in a propane generator to have on hand in case of any kind of power shortage.

Powersheds

Powersheds are mostly used for solar and wind power. When generally you would have solar panels hooked directly up to the house, a powershed allows you to keep all the necessary components of a solar or wind power generation system away from and off of your house. You might consider a powershed if you do not have a very large home to place solar panels on or do not have a basement to store certain components in.

The energy is collected and stored using the powershed. The energy is then run to the dwelling via underground piping. The powershed is then hooked up to a circuit breaker within the home to control the power.

Reduced Energy Consumption

There are some very simple and basic things that you can do to reduce your energy consumption, whether or not you are off-grid. You probably already have heard of the basic things like shutting the lights off when you are not in the room, turning off and unplugging your electrical appliances when you aren't using them and so on. But what are some of the things that you can do specifically to reduce your energy consumption?

While living off-grid, you are probably a little more conscious of your energy expenditures. If you use too much energy while living on the grid, the only consequence is a higher energy bill. If you are using too much energy while living off-grid, especially if you are completely disconnected from grid power, it could result in a total blackout until more energy becomes available from your energy source.

Using LED lights are a great way to save on the use of energy in your home. You can also invest in some smart and automated home devices to help turn off lights and appliances if you have a hard time remembering to turn things off. And, of course, always turn off your lights when you are not using them. Where you place your lights can have a big effect on your energy use as well. You can also use the walls in your home to reflect light.

Use natural lighting to your advantage, not only with using solar power systems, but also just by getting more natural lighting into your home. You can use natural lighting and sun to your advantage for heating your home as well.

Heating and cooling your home can use up a lot of your energy sources. Keeping your windows open in the summer can help to keep your home cool. If you are building your home, window placement can be a very important factor to consider. Which way does the sun shine in? Where can you get the best breeze? And so on.

You can also use a wood burning fireplace in order to heat your home during the colder months. A wood-burning stove is also an option but does require having the availability of wood and a lot of manual labor to split those logs up.

Ensuring your home is properly insulated can also greatly reduce the energy expenditure for heating and cooling your home. A good installation system can save as much as 40% to 50% on energy costs, or in this case, savings. Proper installation can also help to prevent condensation in the home which inhibits the growth of dangerous molds.

Appliances can be a huge energy suck and tend to use a lot more energy than your lights. Make sure to unplug them when you are not using them. This doesn't just mean turning your TV or computer off, this means completely unplugging it. Appliances still use energy when they are plugged in even if you are not actively using them.

If you are using a DC power source as we discussed before, such as a solar power system, then opt for more DC powered devices, this will help to eliminate the need for power inverters.

Chapter Summary

While there are several different kinds of energy sources that you can use when going off-grid, which one you choose will highly depend on your available natural resources. Solar power is a very popular option but can be pricey to get started for a large property and energy production decreases when there is not much sunlight available. Solar power is a great compliment to use with other systems and can store a lot of excess energy in batteries. Solar power can also be used in just about any location, whereas other forms of alternative energy need specific natural resources.

Wind power is a great complement to solar power. It is very inexpensive to get started with and a small turbine can provide a good amount of power. If you need more power, however, a much larger turbine is going to require a lot of space and money to get started.

Geothermal power draws upon heat from the ground and utilizes that to heat a dwelling. It can also be used in addition to other forms of alternative energy and used in just about any location. It can, however, be pricey to get everything installed.

Hydropower is a great option if you have fresh running water on your property, like a river or stream. Hydropower is great because it runs 24/7 and is very affordable to get started with. The biggest downfall is being able to find a property that has running water to utilize hydropower.

Propane is a very cost-effective, readily available,

clean-burning fuel. Propane, like other alternative energy sources, can be combined with other sources. Propane is great for cooking and heating your home.

You can utilize a powershed, that is located away from your home, to house solar panels, piping, and other components of your alternative energy system. This is useful if you do not want solar panels directly on your home or it is not large enough to put panels on.

You can easily reduce your energy consumption by implementing various energy-saving habits including:

- ☒ Shutting off lights when you are not in the room
- ☒ Unplugging all electronics when they are not in use
- ☒ Using LED light bulbs
- ☒ Using natural light to your advantage
- ☒ Ensuring your home is well insulated
- ☒ Using energy-saving appliances
- ☒ Switching to DC-powered appliances

In the next chapter, we will talk about how to stay in touch with the outside world while living off-grid.

CHAPTER SEVEN:
Communicating With The Outside World

People seem to have this misconception that if you live off-grid that you can't have any connection with the outside world.

When I used to hear the term "off-grid", I would picture this old man with excessive facial hair living in his run-down cabin, drinking the coffee that he made over his wood-burning stove while reading newspapers that were decades old because he was so disconnected with the outside world.

Hear me on this...

You can live off-grid and still stay connected.

Especially if you plan on making a living while living off-grid that does not require you to leave your little slice of paradise and commute to a 9-5 in the city. If going off-grid meant that you couldn't stay connected, living off-grid would not be possible for many people as they work from home and rely on being connected online.

You can still remain connected to the outside world while living off-grid via cell phones, internet, and satellite TV. You can even use signal boosters so you don't have to return to the stone age of dial-up internet.

Cellphones

While most days I prefer not to be on my cell phone, it is nice to have to stay connected with my friends and family. To clear something up right away, just because you can get internet service in a location does not mean that you can also get cell phone service. While there is no guarantee that you can get cell phone service in any location, nor that you won't have to stand outside holding an antenna when making a call, there are options for off-gridders that are in fairly remote locations.

If you don't already get a cell phone signal where you are located, you can look into getting a cell phone signal booster. Most cell phone signal boosters can get you full bars with 4G service. These boosters should get you better working phones and cellular devices, such as tablets, hotspots, and laptops. A cell phone booster is also not restricted by your service provider and is very easy to install. Even better, there are no monthly fees and no need to connect to your WiFi. You can even use cell phone signal boosters for cars, RVs, boats, and other mobile vehicles.

Simply do an internet search for "cell phone signal boosters" to find one that will work for your needs and budget.

Internet Options

There are several different ways that you can get the internet to your off-grid home. The type that will work best for you and the signal strengths you can obtain will greatly depend on your location.

Satellite internet

One of the most common solutions for off-grid internet is via satellite. While satellite internet is not going to be as fast as your traditional internet you would get in town, it is still better than dialup and certainly better than nothing. Having satellite internet is really amazing, but don't go into it with unrealistic expectations.

After all, your signal is being sent up to space and back, that is a very long way. There are satellite internet options that are using some great technology to help give you faster speeds. The most common satellite internet speeds are 25 Mbps for downloads and 3 Mbps for uploads, which is still enough to stream music and movies. You are also able to use WiFi while using satellite internet, which is great if you want to use a laptop, tablet, or any other wireless devices.

Use your cell phone

If you are in a location where you get pretty good cell phone service, you can certainly use your smartphone for many applications. While I wouldn't suggest using your cell phone to write a book (believe me I've tried, it's not very easy), you can use it for many other things like paying bills (if you have any), streaming music and movies, and connecting with friends and family. Heck, I know people who live on the grid and just use their cell phones for all of their internet needs.

If you only need to connect to the internet using a computer once in a while, you can still use your cell phone. Simply tether your laptop to your phone's hotspot and you are good to go. Often times speed coming from your mobile hotspot on your phone will be a little slower but should still be manageable. Using a hotspot often is not a big deal if you have an unlimited plan on your cell phone, you just need to be aware of the limitations of your unlimited plan, because realistically, unlimited doesn't really mean unlimited.

Cell phone booster

I mentioned cell phone boosters in the previous section for getting reliable cell service. You can also use a cell phone booster to get wireless internet through a cell phone provider. By connecting to the provider you can get 3G or 4G internet just like you would on a cell phone. The nice thing about cell phone boosters is that you do not have to pay an extra monthly fee for internet service, so you can get away with just paying one bill to a cell phone company.

Fixed wireless broadband

This is a great option for rural communities. This type of internet does not go through a cell phone provider or a satellite but rather uses antenna radio waves. When you sign up for fixed wireless broadband service, which is operated by private companies with antennas in rural areas, you are connected to the host antenna via radio waves from an antenna that is installed on your property. The biggest thing is that each antenna must have a line of sight with each other. The signal from your antenna will run to a WiFi router to your house and you will get the internet. While this is one of the slower options, it is a reliable one.

Free internet

If you are not set on having internet directly in your home, you can always use free internet in public locations such as coffee shops and restaurants. I used to do this all the time when I first started my off-grid lifestyle. I would schedule some work time at a coffee shop in the closest town. While it was kind of a pain not having internet on-demand, it saved me a lot of money in the beginning.

Unlimited membership plans

There is a third party company, named Unlimitedville, that buys big chunks of data from the four major cell phone providers and sells unlimited data to customers via a membership plan. This is a great option for unlimited plans that is reliable and provides truly unlimited internet access. With this plan you don't have to worry about data caps or weather issues like you would with a satellite provider.

Satellite TV

If you are already getting internet service to your home, then you can easily use wireless streaming services to watch TV. You can also get TV service through satellite television just like you would with internet service. Or, you can go old school and just buy movies you want to watch.

If you do decide that you would like to pay to watch TV, there are many different satellite TV services available. Just remember, that it does take electricity to run the TV just like any other appliance.

Signal Boosters

As I mentioned in the cell phone section above, using a signal booster to help to get cell phone service and wireless internet to your property when you otherwise would not have been able to get reliable (or any) service, is a great option.

Signal boosters can be used in a homestead, RV, cabin, or even a houseboat. You can even use them while camping or hiking. They are small, portable devices that can boost the signal of multiple phones, simultaneously within a close area. Many boosters work with all major cell service providers and will get you 4G service.

If you are an RVer or live in a home that is often on the move, boosters are a great option. You can easily install a booster in your home or vehicle (or both) in less than 30 minutes.

The signal booster works by taking the cell signal from outside and amplifying it and rebroadcasting it inside your vehicle or dwelling. This allows you to be farther away from cell towers without losing your connection.

Chapter Summary

Living off-grid does not mean that you need to be a hermit from the outside world. You can enjoy the independence of living off-grid while still enjoying the modern pleasures of the internet, cell phones, and TVs.

If you can not get good cell phone reception, using a signal booster can help keep you connected to friends and family as well as offer reliable wireless internet service. You can get internet through your cell phone, a satellite internet provider, or fixed wireless broadband service. Your TV needs can be satisfied via satellite

TV, streaming movies and TV shows via your internet service, or just buying DVDs to use.

Using a signal booster is great for any type of dwelling, whether it be mobile, like an RV, or a larger property like a homestead. What is available will greatly depend on where you are located. Do some research beforehand to find out what services are available in your ideal location.

In the next chapter, we will review how to create a self-sustaining food system for your off-grid lifestyle.

CHAPTER EIGHT:
Sustainable Food Sources

W E ALL NEED to eat!
In my opinion, one of the best things about going off-grid is the sustainability factor. It doesn't really matter what is going on outside my little slice of paradise, I know that I am taking care of myself and I can sustain my lifestyle.

With all that is going on in the world, sustainable food sources are so important! There is nothing quite like having a meal that you made from food you grew, raised, or caught.

In this chapter, we are going to take a look at farming and homesteading a self-sustaining ecosystem, how to can and preserve foods, as well as hunting and fishing for food.

Farming And Homesteading

Take a minute to think about what life was like before fast food chains lined the main streets of the world; before you could call and order food and have groceries delivered to your door; before there were vending machines and coffee shops at every corner.

People had to plan, they had to grow, they had to harvest, they had to hunt and gather.

While living off-grid does not mean that you can't run to the grocery store when you need something. It is about being more conscious about where your food comes from, how it is made, and how it is processed. Most off-gridders opt for using their own sustainable food sources. You can grow, harvest, and hunt/fish just about everything you could ever need.

In order to create a self-sustaining food source, you must be able to farm and homestead or raise livestock for your main food sources. You don't need a ton of land to farm on. You can grow all the food you need on as little as a half-acre of land. Subsistence farming is the practice of growing all of the food that you and your family will need to survive, with crops and livestock being your primary food sources.

By nature, homesteaders are usually organic farmers. Many homesteaders practice shift farming. This is a technique in which you farm on one piece of land, then shift your farming practices to another piece of land so that the first piece of land has time to recover to its natural state and has time to rest. This can also be done on smaller plots of land.

Depending on how much land you have to use for farming, you can grow a ton of food, even in smaller spaces. What you grow for food will depend on what your family enjoys eating. There are some common staples that you should consider growing. Some of these staples, like beans, you can dry or can and store for long periods of time. Some of the common staples that homesteaders grow are:

- ☒ Greens, lettuce, spinach, etc.
- ☒ Carrots
- ☒ Onions
- ☒ Beans
- ☒ Peas and other legumes
- ☒ Potatoes
- ☒ Tomatoes
- ☒ Corn
- ☒ Herbs and medicinal plants
- ☒ Beets
- ☒ Peppers
- ☒ Cucumbers
- ☒ Fruits and or nut trees
- ☒ Fruit bushes, like berries

Many of these foods can be canned and stored for use over the winter. Or, you can continue your farming in a greenhouse when it gets too cold outside. I know people that will produce vibrant, healthy crops during the dead of winter in the northern states and Canada. It comes down to trial and error and planning.

What you grow can also depend on your location. Things of a more tropical nature will do better in places with year-round warmth. Although it is not impossible to grow tropical foods up north, again, this is where a greenhouse comes in handy.

Livestock is also a great option for feeding your family. It takes a little more money and planning to include livestock on your homestead, but it is well worth it. Livestock can include animals that you will eventually slaughter and use for meat or that you use to produce food - cows for milk, chickens for eggs, and so on. Some of the more common livestock for homesteads includes:

- Cows
- Pigs
- Chickens
- Goats
- Ducks
- Rabbits

The wonderful thing about livestock is that you can start breeding them. This means your investment might be a little more upfront, but if you have livestock that keeps breeding, then you essentially have a never-ending food supply. There is a bit of a learning curve with some livestock though, especially if you are considering breeding, so make sure you do your research before you just throw some animals together and expect them to make more livestock for you.

Having dairy cows or goats can also produce milk, cheese, and other dairy by-products. Cheesemaking is a fun hobby and can be very lucrative if you decide to sell your goods at a farmer's market. With access to fresh milk you can make cottage cheese, mozzarella, sour cream, farmer's cheese, mascarpone, heavy cream, ricotta, and so many more. Many of these are very easy and fun to make.

If you are using livestock for meat, you can slaughter the livestock for yourself (or take the livestock to a butcher) and freeze or jerky the meat for use throughout the year. On average, a steer that weighs 1,000 pounds will yield about 430 pounds of meat. That is plenty, even to feed a large family.

Furthermore, when you are growing and raising your own food, you know where it is coming from and what is going into it. You don't have to worry about consuming meat that has been pumped full of hormones or veggies that have been sprayed with pesticides. This not only equals a healthier environment, but it also equals a healthier you. Also, your livestock and your fruits and veggies can help to feed one another. Your animals can fertilize your plants and any excess plants you produce - or scraps you would normally throw away - you can feed to your animals. It's a beautiful symbiotic relationship.

Then there are bees and honey.

Beekeeping is a great hobby, great for your farming practices, great for the environment as a whole, and of course, the honey and other benefits of beekeeping are delightful. Beekeeping can produce honey (the best you have ever tasted), beeswax, which is great for candle making and also making natural cosmetic products, and propolis, which has some incredible medicinal benefits.

While beekeeping can be a little intimidating when you first get started, there are many resources available online where you can get complete kits to get started for a very affordable price. Beekeeping is a commitment though. There is a lot to learn about bees in order to be successful with them.

With farming, livestock, and beekeeping, whatever you overproduce, you can sell at local farmer's markets to make some money to keep your homestead running. People love to buy local honey and are willing to pay premium prices for high-quality food that is ethically raised.

Canning And Preserving Foods

Unless you can farm the entire year and are only producing the exact amount of food that you need, you are going to have to can or preserve your harvest. You can easily can foods by placing them in a jar and using either a pressure canner or a water bath.

While freezing your produce is certainly an option and might be better for some types of produce than for others, many people prefer to can food for several reasons.

Canning food provides a flexible storage space. You don't have to worry about trying to fit everything in your freezer, you can easily move canned foods around. Not to mention they are great for sharing!

One of the biggest appeals to canning your harvest is that once it is canned it does not continue to use your energy resources like frozen foods would. If you ever experience a power outage, you don't have to worry about all of your frozen foods going bad.

Canned foods are also very easy to use. You don't have to worry about taking something out of the freezer and thawing it ahead of time if it is canned, simply pop the jar open. Canned food also tends to taste better and preserves a greater amount of nutrients.

Canned food also incurs less waste. You aren't storing your foods in large, plastic freezer bags. You are storing your food in reusable glass jars. Once you have used the item, you can clean out the jar and reuse it.

Using a water bath, you can use the old fashioned method, which only requires a large pot, some water, a burner and sealable glass jars - often items people already have on hand. Not to mention, canned foods can last for a very long time. While it is recommended that home-canned foods be consumed within a year of being preserved, some foods can last even longer than that.

You can also grow foods that don't need to be processed in any way to preserve them. Greens such as kale, collard greens, brussels sprouts, and cabbage are good staying in the ground almost until they are covered in snow. While these veggies might not be great to eat raw once it gets cold out, they are still great cooked, not to mention packed with nutrients. Vegetables such as carrots, potatoes, sweet potatoes, pumpkins, onions, leeks, winter squash, parsnips, radishes, beets, garlic, and pretty much any root vegetable will last a very long time in cold storage such as a root cellar.

Hunting

If you have a large enough plot of land that you are able to hunt on, this will open up a whole other sustainable food source for you. While hunting for many is a hobby and enjoyable pastime (known as sports hunting), those living off-grid use hunting as a reliable food source to provide for their families.

Hunting wild game can include turkey, deer, quail, foxes, rabbits, ducks, and other wild game native to the area. If you are not a hunter by nature, it can take some time to learn how to properly hunt. You can't just walk into the woods with a gun or bow and arrow and expect to bring home dinner if you have never done it before.

First of all, check with local ordinances if you need

any type of permit or license to hunt or fish on your own land. Secondly, check to see if there are required hunter's safety permits required (which you should do anyway if you have never hunted before).

There are several tactics and practices that you can use to get the most out of your hunting venture. Deer bait, for example, can be corn, peanut butter, sugar beets, salt, acorns, and vegetables. Baiting is the practice of placing bait around the animal's natural food source. This is generally done in an open area where you can effectively kill the animal.

The Battue practice is something often seen in movies but is a very old technique. It often requires a group of hunters, one that rustles some bushes or bangs branches together to scare the animal out of hiding. Then the second hunter traps or shoots the animal.

Animal calling is another popular method that is used by game and homestead hunters alike. Game calls are man-made devices that look like a small instrument. The sound that comes from the call depends on the animal you are hunting, there are different kinds of calls for many different kinds of animals. A call is often used in addition to other hunting techniques.

Stalking and tracking are two of the oldest methods of hunting which were perfected by our ancestors. These methods take a lot of skill and knowledge about the animal. The hunter must use the natural environment, such as trees, branches, mud, and water to determine where the animal is moving to, track it down, and kill it.

For smaller prey, trapping is a great and fairly low energy option. Buy some traps, or if you are really ambitious you can make some, place them where the animals are, and wait. Check them the following day, if you have a trapped animal, you have dinner. While this is great for things like rabbits, trapping deer might be a little more difficult.

Trained hunting dogs can also be used to help flush out prey or retrieve during a hunt. Dog breeds such as pointers, retrievers, spaniels, hounds, and pitbulls make both great companions and great hunting dogs.

Fishing

If you have access to a freshwater stream or river on your property, you have the best of both worlds, access to unlimited hydropower and fish! Unlike the learning curve and manual labor that goes into hunting your food, fishing, by comparison, is pretty darn easy. Fishing is actually one of the most common sustainable and off-grid food sourcing practices in the world. Fish is also one of the healthiest foods as they are packed with vitamins, minerals, and healthy fats.

You don't need a big fancy boat or loads of expensive equipment to source a lot of fish. Artisanal fishing is the opposite of industrial fishing. It is a small scale operation that is often used to catch fish for food for a family or small community.

While often people think of fishing as sitting on a boat for hours and catching maybe a few tiny fish, there are many ways to fish for food for your homestead. Of course, there is the traditional fishing pole method using a hook, tackle, and bait. Simply toss the line in and wait for the fish to bite. While this might be fine if you are only feeding one or two people, this is not really a sustainable method to feed a larger family. Unless of course, you have a stocked pond with a TON of fish or a stream with fish just waiting to jump out into your frying pan.

The purse seining method can be very effective for catching a lot of fish at once. This method does require at least two people. The "purse" is a net with a string wrapped through it. The fishermen wade in the water and wait for a large group of fish to swim into the purse then quickly raise up the string to create a "purse" full of fresh fish! This is a very effective method to use in a river or stream with shallower water, not too deep to stand in.

Gill nets are similar to a purse net but used for deeper waters and are often strung between two boats. While this can be very effective for catching a lot of fish, it is not very practical for a smaller homestead. Such nets can also trap and harm species such as turtles in fresh and salt waters and ocean-going mammals in the seas.

Traps and pots are great to use in ocean water to catch lobsters and crabs as they can be placed on the ocean floor. Traps can also be used in lakes and ponds to catch smaller species of fish or shellfish, like crawdads.

Even if you do not live by a body of freshwater or

saltwater, you can still get access to fresh fish via an aquaculture fish farming system. This is a large tank of water where you are actually farming fish, so you never have to worry about running out.

Meal Planning

With the abundance of food that you will be producing and catching, meal planning is very important. You simply can't run to the corner store to grab a frozen pizza if you don't have any groceries left. Also, you are not going to want any food to go to waste. Meal planning while living off-grid is very similar to meal planning in the traditional sense in that you need to plan your meals, gather your ingredients, prep your meals, and eat them.

One of the biggest differences here is that you plan your meals based around the food you are producing at your off-grid location. For example, if you have recently had a pig butchered, then you would include a lot of recipes with pork. Off-grid meal planning has a lot to do with seasonal eating as well. While you probably preserve and can various fruits and vegetables, most of the fresh fruits and vegetables you consume will be seasonal. For example, you are not going to be meal planning a meal with fresh strawberries in the middle of a Wisconsin winter. Although something with frozen strawberries or strawberry jam would be fine.

Eating seasonally has many benefits as this is how our ancestors ate. While there were primitive food preservation methods, there were no freezing and refrigeration to save foods. Seasonal eating is also better for you as you are able to consume the foods in their freshest forms. This means that they have the highest nutrient and mineral content.

Many homesteaders and those living off-grid rely on bulk buying things that they do not produce, such as sugar or flour.

One of the biggest differences with meal planning living off-grid is how you start the meal plan itself. You have to ask yourself, what do I currently have to use rather than what am I hungry for that I can go to the grocery store and buy?

When creating your meal plan, you should start with whatever is fresh and what you have an abundance of. Next, what do you have available that needs to be used up quickly that might go bad soon? Also take a look at what you don't have very much of that you shouldn't be using in your meal plan until you get more of those items.

You can choose to meal plan for a week at a time or even a month at a time depending on how much food you have available.

Chapter Summary

Living off-grid sustainable food sources are a must. These sustainable food sources can include farming, hunting, fishing, raising livestock, beekeeping and even aqua-farming fish.

Farming practices can take place in just about any location and even in the winter months if you have a greenhouse available. You can preserve your harvest by freezing or canning your fruits and vegetables. You can also sell any excess that you produce to help make money to sustain your off-grid lifestyle. What you can effectively grow will depend on your location.

Adding livestock to your homestead, especially if you decide to breed the animals, is a great way to create a sustainable source of food for your family. Beekeeping is a great hobby to take up while homesteading and provides many health and environmental benefits.

Hunting and fishing are also great options for sustainable foods on your homestead or off-grid living situation. Both provide a wide variety and can produce a lot of food, even to feed a big family.

Now that you have figured out how you are going to get water, electricity, internet, cell phone service, TV, and food to your off-grid home, let's cover everything you need to know about keeping it safe from evildoers or zombies.

CHAPTER NINE:
Keeping Your Homestead Safe

A FTER ALL OF the hard work that you put into building your perfect off-grid home, you want to be sure to keep it safe. Intruders, bears, the government, whatever you feel may be a threat, there are ways to protect yourself. Location can play a big part in your safety and your visibility. It is great to be able to see out from your property but for people not to be able to see you very well.

There are several things that you can do to protect your family and your property, such as the use of gates, cameras, dogs, and knowing your neighbors (no matter how far away you are from them). While you certainly can choose what will work best for your property or dwelling, you can also layer your security measures to provide more protection for your home and family.

Gates

If you already have a property and can't move to your ideal location where you can see any impending danger coming, there are a few simple things that you can do to start protecting your property. Particularly if you are in a wooded area and have a spot to put up a gate, that is a great deterrent for people attempting to enter your property. If possible, position the gate so a vehicle can't really get around it, use large stones to block the sides or drop off areas.

Leaving a gate open won't necessarily give people the open invitation to enter your property. Locking things can also signal that someone is home and you should not enter the property. You can also place signs in the entrance of your property to indicate that it is a private property and people should not trespass. "No trespassing," "surveillance cameras," and "beware of dog" can really help to deter people from entering your property.

You can actually install multiple gates if you have a very long driveway, one closer to the road and one closer to your home for an extra level of protection.

If you prefer to keep your gates closed and don't want to have to get out of your vehicle every time you want to open them, you can consider adding a solar-powered automatic gate opener. These are great because you can install them on very large, homestead type gates and it doesn't require any electricity to run it other than a dedicated solar panel. The most popular options include a large control arm that is powered by the solar panel and made to open and close with a simple device that looks like a keypad garage opener.

There is also an option to install a large locking mechanism to lock and secure your gate so people can't just push the gate open. When you open the gate, the large lock will disengage before the control arm opens up the gate. You can also install an electro-magnetic sensor that will open the gate when you drive up the driveway to exit it. You can also set the gate to auto-close after a certain amount of time, giving you plenty of time to safely drive out of the gate.

Fencing

Fencing, while great for keeping animals safe and where they should be, is also important for security purposes. If you have a large property, fencing the perimeter can help to deter unwanted animals and people and also signal where your property starts and ends.

But before you grab your post hole digger, make sure that you are checking with local ordinances to ensure that the type of fencing and the placement of the fencing are going to be both legal and effective. If your property is not already fenced, installing fencing can be a large expense and a very time-consuming project. Especially if you are keeping animals, fencing should be a top priority in setting up your off-grid homestead.

When installing new or fixing up an existing fence,

you need to make sure to have everything mapped out. Figure out where the fencing is going to go, if you are having different types of fencing for different areas, and if you need to add additional gates for security or animal safety. You can easily do this by drawing out a map of your property or getting an aerial photo to help determine where you are going to place everything.

If you are keeping a variety of animals, it is a great idea to keep different paddocks for different animals. This will also allow you to rotate your livestock through different paddocks, which helps to improve the grass management, the quality of the feed, and the overall herd health. Larger paddocks can easily be divided up into smaller sections using solar powered electric fencing.

Having various gates throughout your fencing can help to give you and your animals better access to the property as well as keeping everyone safe. While you shouldn't need more than one or two gates on the perimeter of your property, having lockable gates between paddocks is suggested.

There are several different types of fencing and each serves various purposes. When planning out your property, you should determine which type of fencing will work best for you. For example, if you have small children in your home, barbed wire fencing might not be the best option.

Wood fencing

While wood fencing was great in the old days, as there was an abundance of high-quality hardwood often available, nowadays lots of high-quality wood isn't as easy to come by or is very expensive. Wood that you buy from a typical lumberyard will last 20 years at best, that is with regular maintenance of painting and staining every few years.

Wood fencing is great for smaller areas like riding arenas and keeping horses and other animals separated. Although it may not be an ideal choice for a perimeter fence as it can be very expensive. Depending on the climate and the humidity of the location, full wood fencing can also be a poor choice.

Barbed wire fencing

While a very affordable option, barbed wire fencing can be a little difficult to work with and dangerous for children and animals. It is a good type of fencing if you live in a very humid area or have limited availability to wood. Check with your local ordinances for the types of "legal fencing" you can have on your property. Often barbed wire is the most common type of legal fencing but has drawbacks as far as the safety of humans and animals that come in contact with the fence.

Woven wire fencing

This is great for keeping in smaller or more crafty animals. Animals like sheep, poultry, pigs, and goats (if you have never had a goat before, they are VERY smart and figure out ways to get out of fencing), woven wire fencing is ideal for keeping them contained. Woven wire fencing is also good for horses and they can't get tangled or hurt themselves as easily in it. It can also help to keep out predators and can last for up to 20 years with minimal maintenance. Keep in mind though that you will also need some strong wooden posts to hold up the fencing.

Electric fencing

Electric fencing is a fairly low-cost option to get started with and is very low maintenance. Electric fencing is safe and does not hurt the animals but, instead, reinforces the herding environment. Electric fencing is great for covering large areas and keeping things on or off of your property. When an animal touches the fencing it sends out short, intense electric pulses that effectively scares the animal away from the fencing.

While electric fencing looks much different than traditional kinds of fencing and should be obvious to humans, always be sure to make your electric fencing readily visible and well-marked to prevent any kind of liability. Electric fencing is also a great option to keep around your perimeter and can be used in combination with other types of fencing to optimize security. You can also get solar-powered electric fencing which is a great option as it will not eat up your energy expenditures.

Cameras

There are many great home surveillance camera systems available. There are a lot of things to consider when installing a home surveillance system such as the amount of property you are going to need to cover, how strong your WiFi signal is, and how much energy you are going to devote to your system.

Game cameras

Game cameras are great to start with and the cheapest option that you can place just about anywhere. A game camera, like you would use for hunting, is often not too expensive. Game cameras are motion activated and take a picture of whatever is moving. While this might not be a great option if it is placed in an area that will get a lot of movement, like on a busy road, it is great to keep in areas that don't have a lot of movement but where you could capture someone trying to do damage to your property (like drunk teenagers taking out your mailbox).

When you are installing game cameras for home surveillance, don't put the camera at eye level. These cameras do very well being high up and people won't notice them as much if at all. Game cameras are also run on batteries and can last for six months to a year on one set of batteries. They are very easy to hide and come in camouflage and green tints to easily hide in trees and bushes.

Game cameras, also known as trail cameras, use infrared technology. You can easily view images using your phone or computer as most models include a micro SD card. Many models can take images from 80 to 100 feet away, allowing you to place the cameras rather far out of sight.

Traditional security systems

Traditional security systems are great if you have access to a landline or reliable WiFi. Traditional systems can be wired or wireless. These systems are also great if you are not very tech savvy and want a plug and play type of system. One of the great things about a traditional security system is that you can operate everything from one central hub.

If you are off the electrical grid, you are going to want to look for a system that is energy efficient and isn't going to suck up all your energy stores.

There are also several options for solar-powered security cameras. Look for weatherproof options that you can keep outdoors all year round and that comes with both day and night vision. There are some models that run all the time and others that are motion-sensitive and will start recording when they detect movement. If you have a smart system, it can alert your phone and start recording whatever is moving and save it to the cloud for access later on.

If you do not have a strong enough signal to connect your cameras via WiFi, you can also get cameras that store to a local SD card, much like the game camera. This will require you to take out the SD card to view anything and footage can be easily overwritten. Depending on the type of security system that you get will depend on the energy that it needs to power it. I would highly suggest a solar powered system as then you never have to worry about outages.

Lighting

Using lighting to be visually alerted by intruders (or the random raccoon) is also a good measure to keep in place. There are many solar powered lighting options that you can use as security lights around your property. You can easily install high powered, motion sensitive floodlights around the perimeter of your home that can be used to light your property in the dark.

Dogs

Dogs, while not only great for hunting and companionship, they are also great for home security. Dogs can see and hear things before their humans take notice, this provides an additional safety mechanism. Essentially since dogs have been domesticated, they have been used for hunting and guarding properties. Speaking in terms of security, dogs don't cost a lot. All they really need is some food, water, and somewhere nice to sleep. There are several breeds of dogs that are natural defenders of their property and their belongings while being loyal to their humans. Keep in mind that many breeds, even ones that are not natural defenders, can be trained to be "guard dogs."

Some of the most common dog breeds that are often used for home defense include:

- ☒ Bernese Mountain Dogs
- ☒ Bullmastiff
- ☒ Rottweiler
- ☒ Doberman Pinscher
- ☒ German Shepards
- ☒ Komondor
- ☒ Giant Schnauzer
- ☒ Rhodesian Ridgeback
- ☒ Kuvasz
- ☒ Staffordshire Terrier

While many of these dogs might not look threatening, they will protect their families at any cost if they feel they are being threatened.

Know Your Neighbors

It doesn't really matter how far away your neighbors are, a great FREE way to help protect your property is to know your neighbors. Many fellow off-gridders have the same types of values and would be more than willing to keep an eye on your property if you keep an eye on theirs as well.

You can even develop a community watch type program or share security measures if you know your neighbors well enough and trust them.

Wireless Security Systems

Wireless security systems are great for very large properties. Wireless solar security systems are great to place around a remote property to help keep up the security level of your homestead. These cameras, much like the solar panels you install on a home, capture the sun's energy and store it in a local battery in the camera and can keep that battery charged full-time. In order to monitor a wireless solar system, you need to have reliable access to WiFi or SIM connectivity to see any captured footage.

Sensors

There are tons of different types of sensors available for just about any location on your property or in your home. Game cameras are a type of sensor. You can also get driveway sensors to tell if someone is driving up your driveway that isn't supposed to be. Driveway sensors can either be motion-activated or cords that run across the driveway and are pressure sensitive.

Vehicles

While having proper vehicles isn't directly related to safety, I wanted to include a section on the vehicles you might want to consider having on your off-grid property to make your life a little easier. Having some kind of truck or SUV (that has four-wheel drive) to haul things will certainly add some value to your life and your property. Something that is able to handle all terrain territory while also being able to haul things like brush, logs, and even animals from one location to another would be very helpful. It is also advised that you have some type of ATV to get into wooded areas and, of course, for a little fun. Having a truck and/or an ATV also allows you to attach a snowplow to the front, which can come in really handy if you live in a location that gets a lot of snow.

If you have a very large plot of land, you might also want to consider a riding lawnmower. While technically not a vehicle, a riding mower can certainly make your task of mowing a couple of acres a lot more pleasurable. If you are living off-grid on a much smaller property, a push mower should be more than enough. Even if living on a homestead, many off-gridders have an RV or camper to take with them when traveling. There is not a large difference in transitioning from living in an off-grid home to using a camper or RV, thus it would make sense to use a camper when traveling rather than staying in a hotel. Also, if you do a lot of traveling, this helps you to avoid having to spend too much on hotel stays.

Chapter Summary

How you set up your security measures will greatly depend on the location of your property and what you have at your disposal. Gates at the entry of your property are a great way to deter people from entering. Try to position the gate the best you can by placing large stones around the outside of the gate so vehicles can't just drive around it. Placing signs around the property letting people know that there is a surveillance system and dogs protecting the property can also help to deter any intruders.

Fencing is not only great for protecting your family but also terrific for protecting your animals and keeping them where they need to be. The correct type of fencing can keep your animals in and predators out. While there are many fencing options available, the most common include wood, barbed wire, woven wire, and electrical fencing. You can purchase solar-powered electric fencing so that you are not eating into your power supply.

While there are hundreds of different types of surveillance cameras to choose from, some of the most commonly used while living off-grid include game or trail cameras and solar-powered wireless cameras that either connect via WiFi or record data on an SD card.

Dogs are also a great security measure. They not only offer protection for your family but can also be used for hunting and companionship. Some of the more common dog breeds used for protection include Rottweilers, Bullmastiffs, and German Shepherds.

Knowing your neighbors is also important. Be sure that you get to know them as you can keep an eye on each others' properties. Placing sensors throughout your property is also important for staying alerted if there is someone trying to get onto your property.

In the next chapter, we will cover all of the different ways that you can make money while living off-grid, from transitioning with your current job to opening your own business. There are tons of different ways that you can make a very good living while living off-grid.

CHAPTER TEN:
Making Money Off-Grid

ANY OFF-GRIDDERS CREATE a fully self-sustainable environment for themselves by also working for themselves or working remotely in some capacity or another. While getting started living off-grid can be expensive, depending on the location you choose and the size of your home and property, sustaining living off-grid can be very cost effective. Although it completely depends on your individual lifestyle.

While many people living off-grid make a living selling things they grow or make there are also plenty of ways that you can work remotely. Off-grid living does not mean having to sacrifice and live hand to mouth, you can make a good income doing things that you are passionate about. I know people who are living off-grid, RVing full-time around the country and are bringing in five-figures per month from their remote work. If you are going to be doing anything online, all you need is a reliable internet connection and the motivation to work remotely.

Working And Living Off Of Your Land

There are many people that choose to live off-grid and homestead. This can include farming, raising livestock, and beekeeping. Unless you have a very large family, many of the products that you produce on your homestead can be sold for a good profit. One of the biggest things about earning a full-time income while living off-grid is still being able to enjoy your off-grid lifestyle. You don't want to be working yourself ragged, 100 hours per week just to make ends meet. That is definitely not the point here!

Farming

Now when I say farming, I am not talking about putting together a local CSA (although that is a great idea if you don't have that in your area and there is a demand for one). Instead, I am talking about produce that is going to give you the biggest bang for your buck. Think about the last time you went to a farmer's market, what did you see there? My guess was that it was all the same stuff - eggs, meats, vegetables. However, there are so many people who sell that stuff it makes it hard to stand out. With so much competition, it can be difficult to make any kind of decent profit. Look for things in your area that are unique that no one else is selling.

Some of the more unique things that I have seen (and even tried) being sold at farmer's markets that do really well are mushrooms, hatching eggs or chicks, honey, maple syrup, medicinal and culinary herbs, and cheeses.

Mushrooms

Mushrooms are a really fun "crop" to get started with selling. They are very interesting to learn about and actually very easy to grow. Fresh, dried, and tinctured medicinal mushrooms sell very well and you can even sell them online. Mushroom farming can also be done just about anywhere and have huge profit margins.

Hatching eggs and chicks

Who doesn't love baby chicks?! If you have some in-demand poultry breeds, you can sell hatching eggs for a few dollars a piece. If you actually hatch the eggs and sell the chicks you can double that price.

Honey and beeswax

I mentioned in a previous chapter the many advantages of beekeeping. Once everything is set up, beekeeping can be a fairly low investment in time and energy. Honey tends to sell very well at farmer's markets and you can also use the beeswax to sell raw or to make into other natural products.

Maple syrup

If you have a lot of Maple, Birch, or Walnut trees on your property you can make a decent income from tapping those trees and rendering syrup. During the winter and early spring before a lot of the other farm work begins, you can work on producing and processing your syrup.

Cheeses

If you have a dairy cow or goat, making various kinds of artisan cheeses can earn you a good income. Cheesemaking, while there is a lot to learn, is very fun. From the very easy - like making fresh mozzarella - to the more challenging creation of artisan hard cheese varieties, there is always room to grow and add more things to make and sell.

Medicinal and culinary herbs

Growing herbs are great because many of the varieties grow vigorously and are natural pesticides. Herbs are perennial plants (meaning that you don't have to buy new seed for them every year and replant them) and they are rather profitable. These herbs sell well in their raw forms, but even better if you can create natural, medicinal products from them.

Renting your land

If you happen to have a very large plot of land and you don't use all of it as effectively as you could, you might consider renting out part of your land to other farmers or homesteaders. This is a great way to earn passive income with minimal work. Just be sure if you are renting or leasing out any land to others that you write up contracts that clearly define the use and associated costs.

Teach homesteading classes

Once you have become very knowledgeable about all things homesteading, you can invite people to classes that you teach on various homesteading subjects. You can easily create a partnership with a local library or community center and either host the classes directly on your land or go to the facility to teach about various topics. This is a great way to earn some extra money while connecting with other like-minded people.

Foraged goods

If you have a very large wooded area on your property and fresh, foragable foods grow in abundance, forage them and sell them at local farmer's markets. You can do this with mushrooms, dandelion greens, and even wild berries. Just be sure that you know what you are doing before setting up a shop with foraged items.

Wood

If you have an overabundance of trees, you can sell firewood and lumber.

Airbnb/Location rental

There are many people that are willing to pay just to stay and camp on your land if you have a nice enough area. If you have a nice large barn that is in reasonable condition, consider hosting as a wedding venue. You can easily charge a couple of thousand of dollars just for a wedding location.

Off-Grid Remote Work

Being able to work remotely off-grid opens up a whole new set of opportunities. As long as you have a reliable internet connection, your possibilities are endless. You can make a good living as a writer, a web designer, and even selling products and services online.

Working Your Job Remotely

Start where you already work. Is your job something that you can do remotely? Or is it possible to transition within your company to a full-time remote position? Or transition to a different company doing the same type of work that accommodates remote employees? There are many companies now that are working towards transitioning full and part time employees to remote positions. In the long run, this saves the company more money as they don't need large offices and can cut back on certain benefits.

Even if your job does not currently offer remote opportunities, you can have a discussion with your human resources department to see if they can make accommodations for you. Unless you are working on an assembly line all day, there are likely many things that you can do, that you already do in your position, remotely. Things like data entry, marketing, and even customer service can all be done either full or part-time on a remote basis.

Freelancing

Freelancing is a great way to start working remotely. It is something you can start while you are still in your full time job and don't need a ton of extra training to do. You can freelance many different jobs, from web design, to voiceover work, and of course, writing.

If you are new to freelancing, you can find jobs for beginner freelancers on freelance platforms and various job boards. Once you start looking, you will be amazed at all the opportunities out there. There are many people living off-grid working as freelancers and making a great income. Some freelance work you don't even need to be connected to the internet all the time to be successful. For example, if you are a graphic designer, you can create your designs and then only need to be online when you are actually emailing your clients and working on web-based applications.

If you are good at writing, freelance writing is a great way to start earning an income online. There are many business owners out there that aren't good at writing or simply don't have the time or desire to write content for their business. You can connect with business owners and offer your writing services to them.

Don't be mistaken, writing is not the only option, there are literally tons of different freelancing options out there. Below is a list of a few different ideas to get you started:

- Social media management
- Teaching/Tutoring
- Interpretation
- Virtual assistant
- Copywriting
- Stock photography
- Ghostwriting
- Translation
- Graphic design
- Music writing
- Computer programming
- Accounting
- Travel consultant
- A Google or Facebook ads consultant

☒ Party planner

So as you can see, there are plenty of opportunities out there for freelance work. Write down a list of things that you are already skilled at and start looking for freelance gigs on social media, job boards, and freelance platforms.

Blogging

Many off-gridders make a living blogging or creating videos on YouTube (more on that in a second). Blogging is a great option for off-gridders because, as I'm sure you can guess, the interest in living off-grid is rapidly growing. People are looking for information about living off-grid from those that are already doing it or have the information they are looking for. Even if you are not living off-grid yet, you can still write about off-grid living topics. All it takes is some research and halfway decent writing skills.

Some great blogging topics to start with are:

☒ How to save money for your dream off-grid home

☒ Raising livestock

☒ Sustainable farming practices

☒ Harvesting and food preservation

☒ Building your own furniture out of pallets

Blogging is also very cheap to get started with. You can start a self-hosted blog for about $100. You don't even have to be super tech-savvy to be a blogger. Many blogging platforms are very user-friendly and easy to navigate and create content.

While you aren't going to start making $1,000's overnight, blogging is a great long-term, sustainable way to make money. If you are going to blog to make money, that is your business, your livelihood. Treat your blog like a business, not a hobby. There is a lot to learn when it comes to blogging, but as with other types of online businesses, learning new things and building your business becomes addictive. The more you learn the more you want to learn.

As with any other type of business, you can make a lot or a little, it really depends on how much effort you put into it.

Blogging can also be a catapult for other business ideas. There are many freelance writers that move into full-time blogging, and then into other ventures like selling goods and services and coaching. One of the traditional ways that bloggers make money is through placing ads on their blog. While this is a great way to start, there are many other ways to make money blogging. Bloggers can get paid by doing sponsored posts, affiliate marketing, selling physical or digital goods or selling services all directly through their blog. Digital products and ads are also a great way to generate passive income.

YouTube

Go to YouTube and do a quick search for "off-grid…" anything, pick any topic, and you will find hundreds of different videos related to the topic you typed in. What this tells you is that there are people out there creating this kind of content because people are looking for it! New homesteaders and off-gridders especially are looking for information on how to do certain things.

Creating YouTube videos is very similar to blogging except that you are creating videos rather than writing. Similar to writing you can make money by creating YouTube videos and having ads placed on the videos, creating videos based on sponsored content, selling digital or physical products, promoting affiliates through your channel and even selling services, such as consultations for people that are starting their off-grid lifestyle.

Some popular video topics include:

- Building off-grid
- Off-grid water sources
- Food storage solutions
- How to plan fencing
- Solar energy
- Converting van, RVs, and other types of spaces into off-grid living spaces
- Pallet projects

- ☒ A day in the life…

- ☒ Sustainable gardening practices

- ☒ Off-grid living in different parts of the country

So as you can see there are tons of different topics that you can cover in YouTube videos about off-grid living. If you are planning on doing YouTube and just getting started, document your journey. People love to watch other people learning from their new experiences and to follow along on their journeys.

Chapter Summary

Living off the grid is such an amazing experience, why would you ever want to leave your slice of paradise to go to work?

While it can take a lot of time and money to transition to off-grid living, you should also have a viable way to sustain yourself and your family after you have made the transition. There are many options to make a good living while living off-grid - from selling the excess from your crops or livestock, to working virtually. Some of the things that you can do to make money off of your off-grid lifestyle are to sell things that you make and produce off of your homestead, such as:

- ☒ Mushrooms

- ☒ Hatching eggs and chicks

- ☒ Honey and beeswax

- ☒ Natural beeswax products
- ☒ Maple syrup
- ☒ Cheese
- ☒ Medicinal and culinary herbs
- ☒ Renting or leasing your land
- ☒ Teaching homesteading classes
- ☒ Foraging goods
- ☒ Firewood and lumber

Working remotely is also a great option. You can see if you can work your current job remotely or transition over to a different company or department that offers remote positions.

You can also do freelance work, start a blog, or a YouTube channel.

Final Words

I T IS MY hope that my story and my knowledge has inspired you to start your journey to your own off-grid lifestyle. While there is a lot to learn and it can take a while to get to where you truly want to be, it is worth it!

Living off-grid is not easy, if it was, everyone would do it. It takes a lot of hard work and dedication to live the off-grid life. There are going to be plenty of times where things don't work out the way you want them to. Things will break, animals will eat produce, threats will happen, but I wouldn't have it any other way. I know that living off-grid is where I am meant to be. And it is my hope after reading this that you feel the same way.

While there are many different types of off-grid living and an even greater amount of different kinds of dwellings, ultimately, you have to figure out what works for you and what is going to make you happy. While some people might feel that roughing it is their dream life, others could not fathom living without running water or refrigeration.

From living in a van down by the river to a log cabin deep in the woods, there is an off-grid option for everyone. But before you drop a couple of grand on a plot of land or an RV to renovate, take some time to really feel out if off-grid living is really something that you can do.

Scope out your ideal locations and go visit them in all four seasons to see what it is like to live there. Try and connect with others in the area and ask them what they like or don't like about living there. Making the move off-grid is a big commitment and not something that can happen over a weekend like a traditional move. This is where determining your *why* is very important. Make a list of all the reasons why you want to transition to an off-grid lifestyle to help determine if it is the right choice for you and your family.

Once you have decided that you are ready to leave "the grid" behind, then it is time to start your transition by downsizing your current belongings and getting rid of all of your junk. It is really amazing how much junk people can collect when they have lived somewhere for an extended period of time. Once you start to get rid of things you will have a whole new sense of freedom that you have never experienced before. Embrace living with the things that you need and getting rid of the things that you don't need.

As I have mentioned a few times in this book, going off-grid isn't cheap, unless you are a single person living in a van, you can do that pretty inexpensively. Transitioning off-grid also means paying down or paying off as much of your debt as possible and saving up as much as you can. Make sure to track your expenses to ensure that you are not wasting money on frivolous items when you should be saving up for the important things to get you to your off-grid lifestyle.

Deciding what type of home you want to live in is only half of the battle of deciding where you are going to live. Unless you are traveling full time, you must also pick a property to live on. Some of the various aspects to consider about a property are the availability of water and how you will dispose of waste (well, septic, stream, etc), how much sun the property gets, where you would place the home (if there isn't one already), and any potential security issues.

Your natural resources are very important, the sun, soil, rain, water, and wind can all help to produce energy for your home as well as food and water. Having access to a fresh and reliable water source, such as a stream, river, or lake is a huge bonus. If you do not have natural running water on the property, you can always drill a well or install underground water storage systems. How to get rid of and process your wastewater can be a lot to consider also. Using greywater for other household functions is a great idea, such as using water from your laundry to flush your toilets.

With anything that you do when going off-grid, just be sure to check with your local ordinances to make sure you are not doing anything illegal and are getting all the proper permits and licenses for your activities.

One of the biggest reasons that people go off-grid

is to disconnect from the utility power grid. Off-grid power can be generated using solar, wind, propane, hydro, and geothermal power sources. One of the advantages of staying connected to the grid is that when you produce more power than you actually need, then you can "sell" it back to the power company in the form of credits. This way, when you experience a time that you are not producing enough energy, you can essentially get your power back from the grid using your credits.

Before you fully transition to off-grid living it is important that you practice energy-saving habits in your current home, such as turning off lights when you leave a room, minimizing your water consumption, and unplugging appliances you are not using.

Of course, living off-grid does not mean that you have to disconnect from the rest of the world. There are many people that live off-grid that still stay connected as if they are living on the grid. You can get cell phone service, use signal boosters, and fast enough internet to still do all the things you currently love to do (like binge-watching the latest Netflix series). In fact, many people living off-grid make a living working remotely. You are no longer strictly limited to dial-up internet speeds and transistor radios when you opt to live off-grid.

And we can't forget about the food. When you live off-grid, it usually means gone are the days of running to a fast food joint because you forgot to go grocery shopping. Meal planning is key, whether or not you are homesteading and growing most of your own food. Your food sources can come from farming, raising livestock, hunting, and fishing, and the occasional trip to the wholesale stores. When you are producing a lot of your own food you have to also be able to preserve food for later use during the offseason. While many off-gridders eat a seasonal diet, it is vital that you are prepared all year round.

Of course, you need to be able to keep your off-grid home safe, no matter where you are. Off-grid security can come in the form of locking gates, various types of fencing, cameras and surveillance systems, motion sensor lighting, dogs, various types of sensors, and wireless security systems. What kind of security you need will depend on your location, your property, and your budget.

Finally, there is the ability to make money while living off-grid. I personally know that I did not want to transition to the off-grid lifestyle and have to commute to my soul-sucking job every day. I chose to work virtually, but there are many different options for making money living off the grid. You can sell what you make off of your land at the local farmer's market and even online. Or you can work remotely like I choose to do. Check to see if your company offers remote work to employees or if you can do the same type of job remotely just with a different company. There are also other options like becoming a freelancer, blogging, and making videos on YouTube.

Whatever it is that you choose to do, just make

sure you are passionate about it. Living off-grid is about building and enjoying your best life. You can't do that while working a job you hate.

So, grab a pen and a piece of paper. Start with your *why*. Then write down your ideal off-grid day, your ideal lifestyle. It can be whatever you want it to be, as long as it makes you happy.

Maybe it is waking up every day next to the beach in your RV and sitting on the seashore writing your latest book.

Or perhaps you are getting up, milking your cow, feeding the goats, and then making videos about your latest homesteading adventure. Whatever it is, it should be uniquely you.

Heck, make a vision board if you have to.

Then after you have down your *why* and what your ideal day and your ideal lifestyle, start working backward. What do you need to do to make that ideal life happen?

You got it?

Good…

Now go out and make it happen!

Resources

12 V Monster. (2016, September 23). Maintaining A Healthy Energy Efficiency In An Off-Grid Home. Retrieved August 28, 2019, from https://www.12vmonster.com/blogs/product-questions/ten-tips-for-off-grid-home-energy

15 Acre Homestead. (2018, January 25). Pros and Cons of Homestead Living. Retrieved August 24, 2019, from https://15acrehomestead.com/pros-cons-homestead-living/

A American Septics. (2019, January 20). WHAT IS A LEACH FIELD? Retrieved August 27, 2019, from https://aamericanseptic.com/what-is-a-leach-field/

Adamant, A. (2017, August 30). How to Earn a Full Time Income While Living Off Grid. Retrieved August 30, 2019, from https://practicalselfreliance.com/full-time-off-grid-income/

Bernier, K. (2019, August 12). 7 Reasons Canning Food Is Better Than Freezing Food -. Retrieved August 30, 2019, from https://www.offthegridnews.

com/off-grid-foods/7-reasons-canning-food-is-better-than-freezing-food/

Dodrill, T. (2018, November 30). 5 Off-Grid Water Sources and Systems. Retrieved August 24, 2019, from https://homesteadsurvivalsite.com/off-grid-water-sources/

Dunn, C. (2018, October 11). Generating off-grid power: The 4 best ways. Retrieved August 28, 2019, from https://www.treehugger.com/sustainable-product-design/generating-off-grid-power-the-four-best-ways.html

Earth Homes Now. (2015). Earth Home Advantages and Disadvantages. Retrieved August 24, 2019, from http://www.earthhomesnow.com/earth-home-advantages.htm

EnergySage. (2019a). How is Solar Energy Stored in 2019? | EnergySage. Retrieved from https://www.energysage.com/solar/solar-energy-storage/how-do-solar-batteries-work/

EnergySage. (2019b, February 14). Solar tax credit – everything you need to know about the federal ITC for 2019. Retrieved August 28, 2019, from https://news.energysage.com/congress-extends-the-solar-tax-credit/

EnergySage. (2019c, May 7). How Does Net Metering Work With Solar? | EnergySage. Retrieved

August 28, 2019, from https://www.energysage.com/solar/101/net-metering-for-home-solar-panels/

Fire Mountain Solar. (2019, March 19). Complete Off Grid Solar System Basics | Living Off The Grid. Retrieved August 15, 2019, from https://www.firemountainsolar.com/learn-more/off-grid-basics/

FosterFuels. (2016, September 1). USING PROPANE FOR OFF-GRID POWER. Retrieved August 28, 2019, from https://fosterfuels.com/blog/using-propane-for-off-grid-power/

Green Energy Futures. (2012, June 10). Geothermal 101 - How to heat your home with just three degrees--Green Energy Futures [YouTube]. Retrieved August 28, 2019, from https://www.youtube.com/watch?v=d85FgaFin2A

Gone with the Wynns. (2014, May 8). How to Prep and Dump a Composting Toilet [YouTube]. Retrieved August 28, 2019, from https://www.youtube.com/watch?v=dYR6GPmDzVM

Guildbrook Farm-Off Grid Living. (2019, July 30). Installing the Best Off Grid Solar Powered Automatic Gate Opener from Ghost Controls [YouTube]. Retrieved August 30, 2019, from https://www.youtube.com/watch?v=iOeqxfW6SOA

Hogan Land Service. (2019, July 26). Everything You Need to Know about Pressure Distribution Septic Systems. Retrieved August 27, 2019,

from https://hoganls.com/services/septic/
pressure-distribution-septic-systems/

Homesteading Family. (2019, May 24). Meal
Planning on the Homestead [YouTube]. Retrieved
August 31, 2019, from https://www.youtube.com/
watch?v=mK0y5XpQUE4

Homestead Village. (2017, September 7).
Downsizing 101: Be Happier With Less "Stuff" |
Homestead Village. Retrieved August 15, 2019,
from https://www.homesteadvillage.org/blog/
downsizing-101-be-happier-with-less-stuff/

Johnson, C. (2014, April 23). How to Live
Off-the-grid in a Tiny House - Shareable. Retrieved
August 24, 2019, from https://www.shareable.net/
how-to-live-off-the-grid-in-a-tiny-house/

Kesler, R. (2019, February 19). This is
How I Get Awesome Water Pressure at my
Cabin | Outdoor Troop. Retrieved August
27, 2019, from https://outdoortroop.com/
how-i-get-awesome-water-pressure-at-my-cabin/

Lorenz, L. (2019, June 14). Off-Grid Security
Cameras: Secure Remote Properties with
No Power Supply & Internet. Retrieved
August 30, 2019, from https://reolink.com/
off-grid-security-camera-buying-guide/

Lyons, S. (2019, January 31). Can You Drive
or Drill Your Own Well? Retrieved August

24, 2019, from https://www.thespruce.com/
drive-or-drill-a-well-tips-4059868

Making Momentum. (2019, May 30). 9 Beginner
Minimalism Tips: Start Simplifying Your Life
(Minimalist Lifestyle). Retrieved August 15,
2019, from https://makingmomentum.net/
beginner-minimalism-tips/

Martin, D. (2019, March 19). Powering the future…
thanks to your neighbor's renewable energy. Retrieved
August 28, 2019, from https://www.renewableener-
gyworld.com/articles/2019/03/powering-the-future-
thanks-to-your-neighbors-renewable-energy.html

Melanson, J. (2016, December 26). 10 Best Dog
Breeds for Home Defense. Retrieved August
30, 2019, from https://www.animalbliss.com/
best-dog-breeds-for-home-defense/

Meissner, N. (2019, February 18). Off Grid
Pressure Tanks. Retrieved August 27, 2019,
from https://www.susprep.com/off-grid-water/
off-grid-water-pressure-tanks/

Memodo. (2018, March 27). Memodo explains the
SolarEdge power optimizer [YouTube]. Retrieved
August 28, 2019, from https://www.youtube.com/
watch?v=V1MQR_IE6gE

Mr. Money Mustache. (2018, May 19). My DIY Solar
Power Setup – Free Energy for Life. Retrieved August

28, 2019, from https://www.mrmoneymustache. com/2018/02/07/diy-solar-power/

Off Grid World. (2018, December 17). How To Find Land For Living Off The Grid - Off Grid World. Retrieved August 24, 2019, from https://offgridworld. com/how-to-find-land-for-living-off-the-grid/

Off Grid Quest. (2015, December 9). Select the best type of fence for your farm with this fencing guide. Retrieved August 30, 2019, from https://offgridquest.com/on-the-farm/ select-the-best-type-of-fence-for-your-f

Poindexter, J. (2017, February 28). Living off the Grid: What Is It and 3 Realistic Options to Start Now. Retrieved August 14, 2019, from https:// morningchores.com/living-off-the-grid/

Powerful Signal. (2019). weBoost Drive 4G-X Portable Off-Grid Cell Signal Booster 470510. Retrieved August 30, 2019, from https://powerful-signal.com/weboost-470510-drive-4g-x-portable-off-grid-cell-phone-signal-booster/

Pure Living For Life. (2017, February 12). How We Researched, Found and Purchased the Best Land For Our Off Grid Homestead. Retrieved August 24, 2019, from http://purelivingforlife.com/ finding-land-for-homestead/

Quinn Farkas, J. T. (2018, November 5). The Off the Grid Living Food Guide - For Growing,

Catching Or Collecting Food. Retrieved August 30, 2019, from https://www.conservationinstitute.org/off-the-grid-food-guide/

Roeder, D. (2017, May 1). Septic Holding Tank Designs. Retrieved August 27, 2019, from https://inspectapedia.com/septic/Septic_Holding_Tanks.php

Rogers, K. (2017, May 10). Pros and Cons of RV Living. Retrieved August 24, 2019, from https://kandacerogers.com/2017/01/25/pros-and-cons-of-rv-living/

Simply Starry Sustainable Living With God. (2016, January 29). Long Term Food Storage Basics: Off Grid Pantry [YouTube]. Retrieved August 31, 2019, from https://www.youtube.com/watch?v=XNsQ_8MKxrw

Solar and Wind FX. (2016, April 8). Off-Grid Cabin/Power shed. Retrieved August 28, 2019, from https://www.solarandwindfx.com/portfolio/off-grid-cabinpower-shed/

Ramsey, D. (2019, August 9). How to Save Money: 20 Simple Tips. Retrieved August 16, 2019, from https://www.daveramsey.com/blog/the-secret-to-saving-money

Riter, S. (2011, December 11). Log Cabin and Log Home Pros and Cons. Retrieved August 24, 2019, from https://theredheadriter.com/2011/12/log-cabin-and-log-home-pros-and-cons/

Simply Starry Sustainable Living With God. (2014, December 23). OFF THE GRID SECURITY~Do It Yourself Home Security Tips [YouTube]. Retrieved August 30, 2019, from https://www.youtube.com/watch?v=fquFOiEsUdM

WatElectrical. (2019, July 23). How Does Solar Inverter Works and Its Applications. Retrieved August 28, 2019, from https://www.watelectrical.com/how-solar-inverter-works-applications/

Wilson Amplifiers. (2019). The Best Cell Phone Signal Boosters for Rural Areas and Farms: The Complete Guide. Retrieved August 29, 2019, from https://www.wilsonamplifiers.com/blog/the-best-cell-phone-booster-for-rural-areas-complete-guide/

Wholesale Solar. (2019). Wind Generators - Compare Wind Generator Prices. Retrieved August 28, 2019, from https://www.wholesalesolar.com/wind-generator-turbines